Overwhelming Odds

To order additional copies, please contact us.
BookSurge, LLC
www.booksurge.com
1-866-308-6235
orders@booksurge.com

SUSAN AND DENNY O'LEARY

OVERWHELMING ODDS

Global Publishing Company
2004

Overwhelming Odds

TABLE OF CONTENTS

Between failure and success the point is so fine,
Men sometimes know not when they touch the line,
Just when the pearl was waiting—one more plunge.
How many a struggler has thrown in the sponge?
There is this honey in the bitterest cup,
The only failure is in giving up.

(Anonymous)

***

This book is dedicated to you - all of you! Those of you who were helping in the limelight; those of you who were praying in the shadows. It is because of you that this tragic story became blessed. It is because of you that we were able to find hope and, at times, even a measure of serenity in the midst of chaos. And it was because of you that the O'Leary family experienced the kingdom of God on earth.

We will never forget your goodness!

INTRODUCTION

This is the true story of a boy, his family, a community, and a
God who persevered against overwhelming odds.

***

PREFACE
We Prepare for the Journey

My husband, Denny, and I had both been cradle Catholics with religious training in grade school, high school, and college. We were even taught by nuns wearing habits. We would not miss Mass on Sunday; we would not eat meat on Friday; and we knew to call a bishop "Your Excellency" and a cardinal "Your Eminence," although we were personally acquainted with neither. Our faith, although real, was stale and not particularly important in our daily lives. As our older children reached school age, we knew that there must be more to teach them than rote prayers, but we knew nothing more and did not spend much time or energy looking for an answer.

Our faith life began to evolve in 1976. We agreed to go on a married couples retreat at Pallottine Renewal Center in north St. Louis County to be given by Father Ken Roberts. Fr. Roberts had gained some prominence through the writing of a book *Playboy to Priest,* which told his story of flying around the world as a British Airline steward before receiving the Lord's call to priesthood.

The only time that Denny or I had been on a retreat was when we were seniors in high school. A retreat is a time away from the normal concerns and pressures of everyday living, where you have the opportunity to reflect and consider where God really fits into your life. The goal of Fr. Roberts' retreat was to attempt to increase the presence and the awareness of the Lord in the hearts and minds of a married couple. The presentation started on a Friday evening and continued through Sunday afternoon. It was excellent. Fr. Robert's reputation as a captivating retreat master was well deserved. There were three noteworthy events, which occurred during or shortly after the retreat weekend.

The first involved some good-natured disagreements with one of my long time friends from high school, who was espousing the joy of having the "Holy Spirit alive in her life." Denny said, "It may work for you, but it sounds like a bunch of pious nonsense to me." However, he confided to me that this friend was somehow different, her enthusiasm was infectious, and her suggestion that we only had to ask for the power of the Spirit, persuasive.

The next incident was connected with our purchase of Father Roberts' book, which he happily agreed to autograph for us. Father Roberts signed the cover and then added, "Remember Susan and Denny, Jesus is alive!" We thought "alive" was a peculiar description. We accepted that Jesus was alive "back then" and that he rose from the dead and is still alive "up there," but we had not experienced Him to be alive in our lives in any "here and now" sense. We could not help but notice the similarity—both my friend and Father Roberts used the word "alive."

The third event took place the following weekend. Another couple on the retreat drove 45 minutes from their home in west St. Louis County to our home in north St. Louis County, merely to drop off a pamphlet entitled "Baptized in the Spirit," written by a charismatic Christian named Steve Clark. They told us that the small book described in detail the actions of the Holy Spirit in the lives of the early disciples and explained that the power was still available—if we only would ask for it.

Denny haphazardly picked up the pamphlet and glanced at it. A few of the lines caught his eye and he began to read it. Before I knew it, he was engrossed in the message and quickly devoured it from cover to cover. The following night he asked me if I would be interested in going with him to the charismatic prayer meeting, which took place every Tuesday night in our parish. Denny and I had been to one or two prayer meetings in the past, but concluded that the unbridled enthusiasm, the uplifted arms, and the shared prayer at the meeting were strange at best, and simply not "for us."

Very reluctantly, I went to the Tuesday night gathering with him. Midway through the meeting, Denny asked to be "prayed over." That was all these zealots needed. He was led to a chair in the center of the room, with hands, arms, and smiles surrounding him. Though somewhat terrified, I was impressed with their genuine joy at the thought of sharing something, which they believed they possessed, in response to Denny's request for the "Power of the Holy Spirit" in his life. Inexplicably to me, Denny claimed to be able to feel the reality of the presence and indwelling of the Holy Spirit. Although there have been some peaks and valleys in his fervor, Denny's faith life changed dramatically and has never again been the same.

During the next few days, I resented this newfound spirituality. I realized that Denny would certainly want to go back to that "crazy" prayer meeting the following week and I felt somehow left out. I decided to read Clark's pamphlet and, amazingly, I was moved by it. I remember thinking "I don't fully understand this, but it seems to be 'real' and if it is, I want it."

The next week was my turn to request prayer for the fullness of the Holy Spirit in a tangible and life-changing way. I nervously headed to the same chair in the center of the room that Denny had occupied a week earlier and timidly told those gathered around that I wanted to be prayed over. A sweet lady leaned over me and asked if there was anything special I wanted to ask the Lord for. I remember hoping to receive the "gift of tongues," which I felt would be the tangible sign that all of this was authentic. However, I did not share that with the group. Only the Lord knew my heart that night. I received the Holy Spirit and the gift of tongues. It was a life-changing experience. I have never been the same.

In the next few years, we became active in the charismatic renewal within our church, recognizing that the enthusiasm engendered by our experience was a starting point only and not an end in itself. Our faith took on meaning, liturgies were exciting, the scriptures became alive, and our knowledge of Jesus Christ as our personal Lord and Savior became the central truth of our existence. We no longer had to worry about what to tell our kids about a Savior who died 2000 years ago. We could tell them about the living, loving, caring Lord in our lives, here and now. Father Richard Rohr, a Franciscan charismatic priest whom we heard initially at a mission in our parish, once said, "Faith is remembering in the darkness what we have experienced in the light."

Denny and I had spent all of our lives in the light with precious few moments of darkness. We were both healthy, our beautiful children were healthy, our parents were all alive, we had a wonderful home, enough money, great vacations and Denny took pride in being an attorney and loved his work in litigation. Faith, prayer, and praise were an integral part of an exciting and blessed life.

However, at times, we were secretly curious, but certainly did not want to know, how we would react if things did not go as well for us. Would we still be able to praise God in the midst of difficulty? Would we still recognize the gift of God's spirit, if tasting emptiness and despair? Ten years after our conversion experience, we were to find out. We found ourselves thrust into a time of incredible darkness. The unthinkable happened, which tested our faith to the core. We experienced first hand the difference between the Jesus of the Resurrection and the Jesus of the Cross. When we are at our weakest, our God can be strongest.

CHAPTER 1
The Happiest Day of My Life

November 22, 2003 was without question the happiest day of my life. This was our son John's wedding day, marking the culmination of a miraculous journey, which commenced seventeen years earlier. The wedding took place in the Shrine of St Joseph, a beautifully restored Catholic Church in the City of St. Louis. We were blessed with an unusually warm day for a late fall afternoon.

Our four daughters, Cadey, Amy, Susan, and Laura were bridesmaids and our older son, Jim, was the best man. Jim escorted me down the aisle to the front row, with my husband, Denny, walking right behind us. As mother of the groom, I knew it was my primary role to wear beige and keep quiet. (Hopefully, John's precious wife, Beth, will agree that I did my best.) Our only grandchild, Kathryn, at age 16 months, decided she strongly preferred not to walk down the aisle as a flower girl, which she communicated by refusing to stand up when the moment arrived.

With the wedding ceremony about to begin, I watched the groomsmen come out to their stations and I reflected on what this day meant. I thought back to a day in October 1988, when my phone rang one afternoon. It was my next-door neighbor, Carol. As we spoke, I watched two small figures running in the backyard. The larger figure bent forward and limped as he ran. I remember Carol saying, "I can't believe how good John looks. He's outside running around again like before. He's going to be fine."

"He's going to be fine"… words that I would never again take for granted; words that I would have given all my earthly possessions to have heard on that fateful day in January 1987—the day that our nine-year-old son John was burned over 98% of his body.

For the O'Leary family, January 17, 1987 is a date forever embedded in our hearts. It is the day that our family embarked on a journey which forced us to come face-to-face with tragedy, ourselves, and our God in a way never before even contemplated.

I set out on this uncharted course with my husband, my injured son, my five other children, my loving family, our special friends, and most notably, the belief and confidence that somehow the Lord would accompany us each step of the way. This book tells the story of that journey.

CHAPTER 2
January 17, 1987—The Journey Begins

January 17, 1987 began as a typical winter Saturday morning in the O'Leary household. The weather outside was bitterly cold and cloudy, with a residual snow cover from the "blizzard" that had dropped some 14 inches on the ground a week earlier. The sun was, thus far, unsuccessful in its effort to pierce the overcast skies.

It was going to be a busy Saturday morning. The first item on my agenda was to take my oldest daughter, Cadey, to her Saturday morning singing lesson. At age fifteen, Cadey aspired to be a great singer, envisioning herself on center stage like a new Barbara Streisand or, at the very least, Whitney Houston. She was the first to acknowledge that much improvement was needed and was the subject of much teasing by her brothers and sisters.

Our seventeen-year-old DeSmet High School junior, Jim, was still asleep in the basement—a retreat by choice—providing a perfect haven for dark, uninterrupted, late sleeping. Amy, age 11, was still dozing; not yet possessed of the requisite energy to officially start her day. Susan, age seven, had made a brief kitchen appearance for a bowl of cereal. She told me she was going to get dressed in her favorite Scotty Dog sweater to which she was proudly affixing her new "Jesus Loves Me" pin. Susan received the pin at church the day before at her first Sacrament of Reconciliation.

I told the girls that I was taking Cadey to her singing lesson and would bring Laura along with me. Laura, our youngest, was 18 months old and adored by her brothers and sisters, as only could be a delightful "surprise,"—trailing the rest of the family by 6 1/2 years. Denny had left home early that morning to prepare for a meeting with two witnesses for a Monday morning trial.

As I entered the family room, I was puzzled to see our nine-year-old, John, standing in front of a blazing fire in the fireplace. Denny would not have made a fire before leaving. John saw the wonder in my expression and proudly volunteered, "I made it!"

I admonished angrily, "John, you should not have done that! You are never to start a fire again by yourself. You are not to get near that fireplace unless either Dad or I am with you. Do you understand?"

John readily agreed, undoubtedly sensing the probable consequences of a negative response.

When I was leaving the house with Cadey and Laura, I reminded John where everyone was, told him I would be back in an hour, and again warned him not to get near the fireplace. Unfortunately, the warning failed to register, because John had some ideas of his own.

Sometime in the preceding fall, John had watched two older boys, playing with fire in a nearby backyard. They sprinkled small amounts of gasoline on an open fire, resulting in a powerful "whoosh" sound accompanied by a brilliant flash of light. This was appealing and did not seem particularly dangerous to the eyes of a nine-year-old, who resolved someday to try it himself.

As I was backing the car out of the garage, John was already rolling a piece of newspaper into an eight-inch pencil thin "stick." He pushed aside the fireplace screen and poked the tip of his paper stick into the fire, setting it aflame. Carefully, protecting the little flame with his cupped hand, he headed slowly to the garage in search of the gasoline. His eyes quickly spotted the large red gasoline container. The gasoline was stored to be used in the springtime, when the riding mower would again be fueled to cut our lawn.

The large container had a five-gallon capacity and was about 2/3 full. It was located in the back corner of the garage on a low shelf. John tried to lift the gasoline container with one arm, holding his burning paper in the other hand, but it was too heavy. He set his burning paper on the garage floor. He only wanted to sprinkle a couple of drops of gasoline on his flame, which had grown larger. John decided that he could accomplish his goal by simply tilting the can over the burning piece of paper to allow a few drops to fall out.

As the container was slowly tipped, and before any of the liquid gasoline began to flow, the heavy, but invisible, gasoline fumes "poured" out of the container toward the flame on the floor.

Gasoline fumes are highly flammable; thus, a river of flame leapt out of the burning torch and traveled upward through the gasoline vapors into the container, resulting in a violent explosion. John, who was bent over the tilted can, was lifted up and thrown against the side wall of the garage, drenched with gallons of burning gasoline. We found out months later that the explosion was so loud that it had been heard blocks away.

With his ears ringing and clothes burning, John staggered through the kitchen to the front hall, screaming in fear and pain. The explosion and John's screams were heard by his two sisters, who raced down the steps and joined in with screams of their own. John's entire body was engulfed in flames.

Susan and Amy, who were sure that they were having a nightmare, yelled for help as loud as they could, unable to do anything more to assist. They watched in horror as the flames began to consume their brother, right before their eyes.

At the same time, awakened by the sound of the explosion, followed by the piercing shrieking of his sisters, Jim raced up the stairs and out of the basement screaming, "What happened?"   Immediately, he threw John to the carpet in the front hall and rolled the carpet and himself on top of his younger brother. The flames would briefly disappear, but would return to re-ignite the gasoline saturated clothing.

Yelling to his sisters to call 911 for an ambulance, and with no concern for burning his own hands, Jim dragged his brother to the yard and rolled him in the snow. The fire was quickly extinguished, but John's body was ravaged. His pain was indescribable. In just these few minutes, John's life had been changed forever. It would never be the same, nor would our family's.

Our home was located less than a mile from the firehouse. During a 2-minute eternity, waiting for the emergency vehicles, Susan made two trips to the kitchen sink to fill a glass with water, which she then threw on John in a seven-year-old's hope of abating the pain and lessening the damage. Thick brown smoke began to envelope the kitchen, requiring Susan's last trip be made to the bathroom sink for a final glass of cooling water.

In the meantime, Amy held John tenderly in her arms, telling him that he would be all right, but fearing that he was so burned he might crumble into ashes. She still remembers how warm his body felt as she embraced him. Jim, when he saw the thick smoke, raced into the house for a second 911 call. When he asked Amy to call for an ambulance, he had not realized that the house, itself, was on fire.

Because the pain was so intense, John cried out to his siblings, "Kill me! Kill me! Get a knife out of the kitchen and kill me."

Seconds later, he cried, "Save me! Save me! I don't want to die. Save me."

When the firemen and ambulance arrived, John was raced to the emergency room at St. John's hospital—about 3 minutes away. Jim, Amy, and Susan stared at each other in shock, not knowing what to do next. With tear-filled eyes, they decided to call their dad at his office.

CHAPTER 3
There's Been A Fire

Meanwhile, as I dropped Cadey off at her singing lesson, I waited for her in the Successful Life Bookstore, a block away. Successful Life was a Christian bookstore owned by a man named Bill Banks. Bill openly shared his faith with friends, strangers, and customers, as a result of his miraculous healing of cancer. Bill had been bed-ridden and given only hours to live, when he was prayed over and received an immediate and complete healing. He had a gentle, easygoing manner and he and his wife, Sue, exhibited a genuine concern for each and every person who entered the shop.

Cadey suddenly appeared in the store, with a look in her eyes which I had never before seen, but which instantly made me feel very uncomfortable. I was filled with fear, and I knew that something was terribly wrong. Cadey, who was always in control of her emotions, said calmly, "There's been a fire at home, Mom. Dad just called."

Cadey either did not know, or did not want to disclose any details concerning John's injuries. I asked Sue Banks to pray for us as Cadey took the baby. We rushed out the door and raced home.

The 10-minute ride home was the longest ride of my life. As we rounded the bend toward our house, I saw a fire engine, police cars with flashing lights, firemen on ladders smashing out the windows on the second floor, and smoke billowing out of our home—the home that I had left just 25 minutes earlier. I looked frantically for my children. A neighbor quickly called to me to tell me that Susan and Amy were at her house. I pulled the car into the driveway and ran toward the house.

Amy and Susan came racing toward me, crying, "John was burned!"

They told me that their dad came home briefly, but then drove to St. John's Hospital, where John was taken by ambulance. Jim said John was burned badly, but, although sobbing in pain, he was able to run and jump into the ambulance.

I asked the children to stay with the neighbors and told them I would call immediately with news of John's condition. My ride to the hospital was surreal. This couldn't be happening to me—to John—to us. As my neighbor drove, all I could say was the name, "Jesus."

I repeated all the way to the hospital, "Jesus, Jesus, Jesus."

When we arrived at the emergency room entrance to St. John's Mercy Medical Center, Denny and our next-door neighbor met me. I saw the despair in Denny's eyes and, as he looked at me, he shook his head and whispered, "Susan, they don't think John will make it."

I cried out, "Where is he?"

I then learned that John had just been taken to what they called the hospital burn unit.

My dad, the senior partner of the law firm where Denny worked, soon learned of Denny's rapid exit from the office and of John's injury, and had arrived at the hospital moments before me.

A woman, who identified herself as the head burn

unit nurse, approached us. The nurse ushered the four of us through a seemingly unending maze of corridors, stairways, and elevators. We walked in silence, each taking refuge in our own thoughts and fears. We followed her to the fourth floor and into the burn unit, where Denny and I were led into a glass-walled room and allowed to see John.

CHAPTER 4
Am I Going To Die?

At first glance, things did not look as horrible as I had feared. John was covered with a sheet. His complexion had a sunburned, ruddy look. His eyelashes, eyebrows, and bangs had been singed off, and I could see obvious burns primarily on the left side of his face and his left ear. But, in spite of what Denny had told me, it didn't appear to me that the injuries would be fatal.

The doctor pulled back the sheet a bit and I saw extensive areas of dry white skin, which did not look bad to me, but which I later learned was the typical manifestation of deadly third degree burns.

John was aware of the severity of his injury. He looked at me and cried. "Mommy, am I going to die?"

John was looking into my eyes for the truth. He did not want false assurances. Here was a mother who winced as her babies got DPT shots, whose eyes moistened empathetically with her children for bruises, scrapes, and falls, and who absolutely panicked when one of them came home late.

With a very calm voice, I asked, "John, do you want to die?"

"No."

I somehow managed words, "Then John, you are going to have to fight as hard as you ever have in your life. You are going to have to run as fast as you ever have on the soccer field.

You are going to have to give it your all and you won't be alone. Know that Daddy and I and Jesus will be with you each step of the way."

It was only after months of reflection that I realized those were not my own words, but a gift from the Holy Spirit, echoing in my aching heart.

John was a unique and wonderful child. His brother and sisters called him "the fine fellow" because he was so happy and easy going. He was extremely athletic, gifted with coordination and an unyielding desire to compete and win. He practiced his skills endlessly in the back yard, often accompanied by his older brother, Jim, who insisted that John dive and leap and do whatever else it took to catch a football, stop a baseball or make a play. John's soccer coach created a special position allowing him to go from end-to-end and side-to-side of the field in order to best utilize his exceptional talents and boundless energy. Accordingly, John understood and appreciated the concept of "playing hard," because that was the only way that he knew how to play.

John whispered, "I'll try, Mommy."

Denny and I were then ushered out of the room and John was left to begin the fight of his life.

CHAPTER 5
Overwhelming Odds

We next were allowed to see John in the late afternoon in his assigned room in St. John's burn unit—a specialized intensive care facility catering to the unique needs of burn patients. We quickly learned that the St. John's burn unit and its chief surgeon, Dr. Vatche Ayvazian, were nationally acclaimed in the field of burn trauma.

When we saw John, we were devastated to the point of becoming numb at the changes that had taken place in three hours. John's little body was wrapped in bandages from the top of his head to the tip of his toes; only his eyes and nose were visible. He was intubated on a respirator to deliver oxygen through a breathing tube and he was receiving fluids intravenously. Large volumes of fluid are pumped into the body of a burn victim during the first 24 hours to help replace the fluid loss caused by the burns and to provide needed moisture for undamaged cells. A tremendous amount of swelling takes place due to the fluid accumulation. John's body was bloated and his head was melon shaped. Although we had been warned about the changes that would take place in his appearance, we were not prepared for what we saw. It was overwhelming.

We had our first conversation with Dr. Ayvazian, some hours after John's arrival at the emergency room. He explained to us the nature and extent of the burn wounds in chilling words and in blunt detail. John was burned on virtually 100% of his body. The center of John's face, a small patch of skin located adjacent to his warm-up suit pocket, a small area under one arm, and his genital area were burned second degree. The soles of his feet were not burned. Every other area, representing more than 85% of John's body, was burned third degree. John's burns were not only extensive, but also extremely deep, extending through the three layers of skin, through the muscle, and, at times, to the bone.

John appeared to be only semi-conscious, but, in any event, could not speak due to the breathing tube and could not open his eyes because of the pressure from the infused fluid. The nurse told us that he could hear us.

We repeatedly told John that we loved him and that we would not leave him. We told him he had a huge mountain to climb and that he would have to take it one step at a time. Denny and I had no concept of exactly how steep and treacherous that mountain would be, or if he would even have the chance to attempt the climb.

We left John's room with Dr. Ayvazian, and I said, "Now Doctor, you've explained to us the severity of John's injuries. Are you saying that he has only a 50% chance of survival?"

Dr. Ayvazian's expression itself gave me the dreaded answer I didn't want to hear.

He said, "Mrs. O'Leary, you do not understand what I've told you. I am not a betting man, but if I were to categorize it in that fashion, I would say that John has less than one half of 1% chance of surviving the night."

The reality, the enormity, and the hopelessness of John's condition and prognosis began for the first time to strike us. These words sapped the very spirit from my heart, literally causing me to collapse into a chair.

I felt as though I had been drained of my very being, and with the aching in my heart that I was feeling, I didn't believe that I had the stamina, much less the desire, to take another breath.

As I later sat alone on that first night, just outside the door to the burn unit, I made every possible bargain I could with God. I prayed for an immediate exchange of persons—allowing me to be the one suffering excruciating pain, swollen twice the normal size, on a respirator—with certain death hanging over my head. I pictured John out there sitting where I was sitting, waiting for me.

I also offered to give up every material thing that I owned, none of which had any value to me now, if John would triumphantly walk through those doors and let me see his precious face once more.

My bargaining, prayers, and quiet sobbing continued throughout the night.

CHAPTER 6
Waiting Room Waiting

The head nurse, who by this time we knew as Cissy Condict, escorted us from the burn unit to the fourth floor waiting room. The waiting room became our home for the next four months, and Cissy would become our primary interpreter of John's treatment and barometer of his progress and setbacks. Cissy dispensed with the usual visiting time rules with regard to our access to visiting John. For weeks, we went into his room at almost any time of the day or night. We later learned from her that this was primarily motivated by the universal belief that John would not survive. She thought that a strong parental presence could significantly help him in his fight for life.

We were amazed at the number of waiting room well-wishers present only hours after the tragic event. My parents, our other five children, my sister and brother-in-law, Denny's brother and sister-in-law, aunts, uncles, doctors, clergy, prayer group members, law firm partners, neighbors, and friends. Saturday afternoon was a blur of meeting, greeting, praying, laughing, and crying, as the crowd of visitors continued to grow. When people inquired as to what they could do, our answer was always the same, "Pray for John!"

We were approached later that day by a woman in our parish with whom we were only slightly acquainted. Her husband, Bob, was in the hospital, dying from cancer. She came to the waiting room to tell us that Bob, when he heard about John's accident and the likelihood of death, told his family, "From this moment, I'm going to offer up all of my pain as a prayer that John O'Leary survive."

We went to Bob's room to thank him from our hearts and to pray with him. He battled the cancer and the pain for four more weeks, until February 17. That extraordinary relationship, though short lived, was one that graced our lives and strengthened us when we needed it most. Bob was one of the first of many of John's special angels.

One of the visitors waiting to talk to us on that first day was Dr. Argyerios Tsifutis, our long-time pediatrician for our six children. As his name might indicate, Dr. Tsifutis was born in Greece, and still spoke with a wonderful, thick, Greek accent. He was our family's doctor for more than 15 years and had diagnosed and treated our children through many a pediatric health problem, covering everything from colic to croup, from earaches to influenza, and from chicken pox to premature fusion of the saggital suture line.

Whenever I asked about a health condition or prognosis, Dr. Tsifutis would explain the diagnosis in detail, suggesting I look through his equipment at ears, throats, or whatever, describing for me, step-by-step, what I saw in an effort to assuage my fears or concerns.

I had always been a worrier of extraordinary proportions. Knowing this, if a condition was at all serious, Dr. Tsifutis would end our session with the promise, "I swear to God, Susie, he (or she) will be OK."

As he spoke, he would make a quick sign of the cross as he mentioned God by name. This pattern of reassurance had become extremely meaningful to a concerned mother of six.

Hoping to have the familiar formula for reassurance

repeated, I took him aside and asked, "Dr. Tsifutis, what do you think?"

He looked at me and said, "Susie, I don't know. Dr. Ayvazian is a very good surgeon." No false bravado, no unmerited assurance, no comforting sign of the cross.

At approximately the same time, my father was receiving a similar discouraging evaluation from his brother, Don Kilker, a long-time physician with outstanding diagnostic skills. He told my Dad, "Bob, just so you are aware of it, John's doctor, Vatche Ayvazian, is one of the best burn surgeons in the country. He himself was burned seriously as a child, and he is passionate about his work."

Uncle Don then added, "I talked with Vatche about John's condition and his realistic chance of recovery. You simply can't expect anything but the worst."

CHAPTER 7
We Place John in God's Hands

A prayer service for John was organized by friends in our parish to take place on this first evening; our associate pastor, Father Jim Edwards, planned to preside. It was a snowy Saturday night. The grade school room mothers used the bad weather telephone chain to attempt to spread the word within the parish school community.

Although neither of us wanted to leave the hospital, Denny thought one of us should attend the church service. I explained to him that I just could not go. In my mind, I was afraid that if I left, John could die. But somehow, if I stayed close, he might stay alive.

When Denny returned, a little over an hour later, he told me that the church was full. We were amazed at the goodness and the love shown by those coming together to pray for our child on that icy, cold winter night.

I learned later that at the end of the prayer service, Denny stood up in the middle aisle of the church and spoke to the assembled group. He thanked everyone present in the church for their concern, telling them that as parents they knew and understood that a child is a gift from God, whom we have the privilege of raising for a while. He said John was such a precious gift to us.

So that the congregation would have no doubt about the necessity of praying for a miracle, Denny explained the nature and severity of the injuries and added that John had no earthly hope for survival. But, with the love of God, and the power of prayer, we still believed he might somehow miraculously survive. At the conclusion of these comments, Denny raised his hands and asked the congregation to join in his prayer:

> *Heavenly Father, we come to you tonight, sad and afraid. You have trusted us with your child, John, to raise and to love. We now place him in your loving arms. We ask you to embrace him, comfort him, heal him, and return him to us. We ask this in the name of your Son and our Lord, Jesus Christ.*

Years later, a friend told me that the congregation left church that night with an unexpected sense of peace—although certainly not from any conviction that John would survive. By 9:30 in the evening of that first horrific day, the visiting room was beginning to empty. Our other five children were leaving to spend the night at my parents' home. Our home was severely damaged, so we would not be able to return for months, which was irrelevant at that time. Denny and I found ourselves alone with our thoughts, our hopes, and our fears. I decided to go to the chapel to pray; Denny went to the parking lot to cry.

CHAPTER 8
Our Sunday Visitors

Denny and I spent the first night on a couple of couches in the fourth floor waiting room; at times, fitfully dozing, but more often, walking slowly back to the burn unit to see if John was still alive. When morning came, we felt emotionless and numb, but exceedingly thankful that John had made it through the first night and had earned a chance at one more day. We knew that the only way that John or we were going to get through this horrendous ordeal was by taking it one day at a time.

Early on that first Sunday morning, we prayed what became our daily morning prayer for John. "Thank you, Lord, for the gift of a new morning. Please Lord, just help John live for one more day. Just one more day, Lord, just one more day."

We attended eight o'clock Mass Sunday morning in the hospital chapel. Father John Carroll, who we eventually came to know very well, asked the congregation for special prayers for a little boy critically burned, who was not expected to make it. He did not know that the "little boy's" parents were present. I'll never forget the Gospel reading that Sunday morning. It was from the Gospel of St. John and recited the need for and promises of getting new skins for new wine. We prayed that this offer of "new skin" was somehow prophetic.

Denny told me that he engaged in a round of Bible roulette in the middle of the night, during a Chapel visit.

Bible roulette, for the uninitiated, is merely holding your Bible, saying a short prayer, and then opening it to a random page as you point to a random line on the page. In theory, it is giving God the opportunity to talk to you. There is not a strong ecclesiastical following for the efficacy of this method of prayer, but regardless, Denny randomly opened the Bible to the Book of John and pointed at the page without looking.

The Bible in question was a Good News edition, which contained occasional pencil drawings depicting the message of the written word. Denny told me that when he looked down, his finger was on a drawing of a body walking out of a tomb covered with white bandages from head to toe, except for his eyes. The accompanying text involved the story of Lazarus emerging from the grave, covered from head to toe with burial cloths. Lazarus was restored to his family, which was our prayer for John.

Was it more than just a coincidence that the Sunday morning reading and the random Bible passage were both from the Gospel of St John? Was it more than a coincidence that the biblical figure in the Bible was dressed exactly like our John and was brought back from the dead, while the other story talked of a promise of new skin? Denny and I were afraid to even hope that we had received a sign.

I called my parents early Sunday morning to report that John had defied the odds and survived the first night. The phone was answered on the first ring with a quick and anxious "Hello."

Our other five children and my parents arrived at the hospital after attending morning Mass. They all expressed the same concern. The phone at their home rang constantly that first night. Every time the phone rang, the entire household would panic—afraid that they were getting "the call" that

John had died. I suggested that we could handle that fear with a simple promise: "If John dies, Daddy and I will not call you, but we will both come home together and tell you in person. Don't be afraid of the telephone."

Two of the girls had nightmares and sleep was fitful at best. Arrangements were made for appropriate medications. We also had to think of making some arrangements for the children continuing with scheduled school and other activities. Although we were on notice not to make any long-term plans for John's future, planning for our five other children had to continue. We decided that I would stay at the hospital for the duration—however long or short.

At this stage, I just couldn't bring myself to leave John, even for an hour. A friend in the administrative section of the hospital was able to find me a room where I could sleep and store a few essentials. It was decided that Denny would stay at my parents' home each night with the children, except for Cadey who would move in with a high school friend.

The fire damage to the structure of our home was confined mainly to the garage and kitchen area, but the entire house and its contents, including the inside of every closet and drawer, were covered with brown soot. Jim and Cadey offered to go by the house, which had been boarded up, to get clothes for everyone to have a week's supply.

About noon on Sunday, a parade of visitors began to arrive; a parade that began on the first day and would continue for months. We were prayed for, and received, remembrance from dozens of priests and ministers from Catholic and various Protestant denominations. We had visits from our friends and neighbors, our children's friends and their parents, from aunts, uncles, cousins, nephews, nieces, teachers, doctors we knew on staff, and numerous other well wishers that had heard about the tragedy and wanted to assure us of their prayers. Although it was difficult to find real joy, a number of poignant things did happen in those unspeakable early days of John's hospitalization.

For example, we had a visit every night for many weeks by John's baseball coach, a young father with two boys of his own. The coach would tearfully promise, "I don't care what they say, Johnny is going to make it; he won't die."

He would then gather himself and his emotions, only to return the next day and once again tearfully assure us, "Johnny is strong and I just know that he is not going to die."

This happened every evening for weeks.

We had a doctor friend visit, whose son was in John's class. He tearfully told us that considering John's significant wounds, the extent of damage, and "certain death" prognosis, if it were his son, he would want him to just die quickly, "But I don't want John to die."

We had visits from my hairdresser in a full-length mink coat, which was noteworthy only because the hairdresser was a man. We had visits from all of Denny's law partners, one of whom collapsed to the ground in grief, as he tried to lift our spirits.

Food and drink were carried into the hospital that seemed sufficient to feed the biblical 5000. One of our friends came by the hospital at 7:30 every morning on his way to work with orange juice and coffee cake, or something similar, to start our day. He would not say much more than, "Good morning; I'll be praying for you and John today" and be gone.

One of our priest friends came by every day to check on us, show support, and usually bring Denny a bag of peanut M & M s.

We had regular visits from a St. John's social worker, who

would start crying as she approached us, tearfully asking if she could do anything. Denny and I would wryly remind each other to be strong for Nancy, to minimize her grief.

Our days waiting in the hospital involved a constant soaking and saturation of our entire family in prayer. Every time anyone would inquire, "What can I do?" Our answer remained constant, simply, "Pray."

A very large number of people inquired; a very large amount of prayers were said.

The fourth floor waiting room became an informal nerve center for hundreds of anxious persons, both in the St. Louis area and throughout many other parts of the country, who were requesting an up-to-the-minute status report of John's condition. The waiting room phone would constantly ring, answered by one of the army of volunteers. By the end of the first week, we had received word from prayer groups from a host of cities throughout the United States, as well as England and Israel, that John was receiving prayer.

Late Sunday afternoon, Dr. Ayvazian came out of the burn unit and said he needed to talk to us in private. Our hearts pounded and our stomachs churned, as we followed him to a room. We had no idea what to expect.

CHAPTER 9
What Lies Ahead

D r. Ayvazian said, "Well, John made it through the first day. He is a tiger. The first 24 hours are so important, but the next 48 hours are equally critical."

A modicum of relief spread over us. At this stage there was a knock on the door. A young doctor, who introduced himself as Tom Vitale, came in. His mother and father lived in our parish. He was to be a key member of the surgical team. He and Dr. Ayvazian worked side-by-side through every one of the operations.

We asked the doctors to explain to us some of the problems that John faced. Dr. Ayvazian motioned the younger doctor back and said, "So many functions and systems of the body are affected by burns. Organs, such as the liver, kidneys, and circulatory system could shut down at any moment. John's enormous fluid loss has created an electrolyte imbalance that could suddenly cause the heart to stop beating. His blood vessels to his extremities (arms and legs) could contract to provide maximum protection to the trunk, resulting in the death and eventual amputation of all limbs. John's ravaged body could get an infection through these open wounds that would quickly and certainly result in his death. John is likely to contract pneumonia. His body temperature will wildly fluctuate due to lack of skin covering, placing him at further risk. That's just a start."

Dr. Vitale then told us that while in the burn center, John would be receiving intravenous fluids containing electrolytes to try to stabilize his heart rate, intravenous antibiotics to try to prevent infection, along with antibiotic ointments and creams, pain medications, and a diet high in protein with nutritional supplements, delivered continually through a feeding tube. The feeding tube would be placed into John's stomach through a tube into his nose to deliver a constant supply of rich nutrients for the body to use in rebuilding.

We then asked what the best-case scenario was. Dr. Ayvazian responded, "The best case scenario never happens. Anything that can go wrong in the treatment of a burn victim frequently does go wrong. Not only were John's burns primarily third degree, but they also exhibited extreme depth, which made recovery an even greater problem. The largest obstacle, the most important requirement, and our ultimate work is to cover John's body again, first covering and protecting the body cavity and internal organs. This will take many months at best.

"We can't talk or even worry about what might happen in six months. We must take it an hour at a time and maybe look forward a day at a time. The first thing we have to do is debride the damaged tissue, which we cut away in order to prevent infection and to provide an area suitable to receive eventual skin grafts. Doctor Vitale and I have scheduled an extensive debridement operation for tomorrow morning. After debridement is complete, we will schedule grafting operations."

But skin grafts require skin. We were reminded that John had almost no available donor sites. The 85% third degree burn sites could not supply any donor skin, but to the contrary, had to all be filled with healthy skin. The doctors planned to take what are called split thickness grafts about the size of a postage stamp from John's scalp, which would then be stretched to extend the use of available skin a little further. This wafer thin skin would be meshed and spread out and painstakingly placed. If all went well, the meshed holes would fill in from all sides and the separate small pieces would grow together with adjoining grafts to once again supply John's body with a protective covering.

We asked about third party skin donations. We said we would be more than willing to donate our skin for John and that we had received a number of other sincere offers of skin from various friends and relatives. The doctor told us that skin from another donor will not take, except from an identical twin. Donated skin from anyone else, even parents or siblings, would be rejected within a few weeks. Dr. Ayvazian's advice was that John would get better results using either cadaver or pig skin to temporarily cover the open areas of his body, while grafting operations were taking place, to provide permanent protection.

Dr. Ayvazian said it was premature to go into any in depth explanation. He said that he anticipated that John would have to survive more than 20 significant operations, including some operations for functional reconstruction at the conclusion of the operations for skin grafting. He would also face some operations on contractures, which could develop. Contractures are a web-like adhering of tissue to tissue, which shorten and take away muscle movement and function. Splints are used to try to curb the development and growth of contractures.

When burns destroy the skin, thick deforming hypotrophic scars form randomly and irregularly. They can be lessened through the application of external pressure. Accordingly, if John were to survive, he would eventually be fitted with tight outer garments to be worn 24 hours a day. He would be required to wear these garments for more than one year.

The meeting concluded with Dr. Ayvazian stating, "Surgery in John's fragile condition is extremely dangerous, but no surgery would mean certain death. We will operate tomorrow."

Tomorrow, if we were given a tomorrow, would be a big day. We decided to conform to the biblical advice to let tomorrow take care of tomorrow, because today had troubles of its own.

CHAPTER 10
Burns

The significance of the statement that John was burned on over 85% of his body in the third degree can better be understood in the context of an explanation of skin—what it is, what it does, and the effect that a burn has on the body's function.

The skin is the body's protective covering. It is actually an organ, just like the heart, lungs, and liver. All bodily organs consist of specialized groups of cells performing vital physiological functions. Skin is the largest organ, comprised of two layers called the epidermis and the dermis. The epidermis is the top thin layer consisting of both a dead portion and a living portion. The main function of this layer of skin is to act as a protective barrier to infections and other outside factors affecting the body.

Glands and hair follicles extend through the epidermis from the lower dermis to the outside of the skin. The dermis is the inner layer of skin, below the epidermis. It is much thicker than the epidermis and contains nerves, nerve endings, blood vessels, sebaceous and sweat glands, and hair follicles. The skin typically rests on a layer of fat cells and is held on by connective tissue.

The skin is capable of amazing healing, reconstruction, and regeneration. However, if burned to the third degree, it is unable to regenerate and medical treatment is required—usually in the form of a skin graft.

In addition to providing a protective shield, the skin performs three other important functions:

1) *Regulating body temperatures.* Humans are classified as mammals, which are warm-blooded creatures. Reptiles, such as snakes and lizards, are cold-blooded. This terminology is not descriptive of the actual blood temperature, but rather describes whether the body maintains its own temperature or whether internal body temperature is a function of external temperature.

The human body keeps itself at a relatively constant temperature in the 98-degree range through the interaction of nerve endings and sweat glands, located in the skin. When the body temperature rises, the nerve endings will make the blood vessels dilate to expose more surface areas permitting the blood to cool. When the body temperature falls, the nerve endings in the skin cause the blood vessels to contract. This results in less surface area and heat retention.

One square inch of skin contains more than 10 feet of these tiny blood vessels, assisting in the task of stabilizing body heat. The lack of these skin-imbedded nerve instructions to the blood vessels would result in wild fluctuations of John's temperature—as low as 91 to as high as 105 degrees Fahrenheit.

The skin is also filled with sweat glands, which, when heated, secrete moisture in the form of perspiration that flows to the body's surface. On the outside surface of the body, evaporation occurs, which then results in cooling. The sweat glands consist of coiled tubes to the outside ending in a pore. In uninjured skin there are a hundred sweat glands per square inch.

John's sweat glands on over 85% his body were destroyed. They could not be replaced or regenerated, which resulted in the inability of John's body to heat and cool properly, creating the risk of heat stroke from temperature or exertion.

2) *Guarding against loss of fluids.* When a burn occurs, the interior muscles and connective tissue are exposed to the air and injury, notably the loss of blood and other bodily fluids, which can quickly cause organ failure and death. The tiny blood vessels in the absence of a burn permit the seepage of blood through the walls to the skin. This is how the skin is kept healthy and alive. When burn damage occurs, the blood vessels enlarge and leak out far too much fluid. Large amounts of fluid must be infused into the body of a burn victim to avoid additional cell death.

3) *Distinguishing between heat and cold and providing other sensory perceptions.* The skin is filled with nerves sensitive to heat and pressure. As a result, we can distinguish between a warm blanket and scalding water, from the tickle of a feather to the impact of a hammer, or to the cut of a knife. The body reacts as appropriate, with a slap at a biting mosquito to a quick involuntary movement away from heat or pain.

Burn Classifications

Burns are classified as first, second, and third-degree, depending on the depth of penetration. First-degree burns are superficial and extend only into the epidermis. The most common example of a first-degree burn would be mild sunburn—slightly painful and red, but no blistering involved. This type of burn will heal on its own in several days. There may be peeling of the damaged skin, but no scarring.

Second-degree burns involve the burn passing through the epidermis and into the dermis. The dermal layer is injured, but the burn does not extend into the underlying tissues. There will be intense pain. If properly treated, second-degree burns will heal within a few weeks, with very little scarring. In a comparison to sunburn analogy, the second-degree burn would result in severe pain, red coloring, and blistering.

Third-degree burns, which are also referred to as full thickness burns, destroy both the epidermis and the dermis. The third-degree burned areas will appear either charred black or dry and white. These burns can, and in John's case did, extend even deeper into the fat cells and down to, or through, muscles and ligaments to the bone. Eighty-five percent of John's burns were third degree. The only treatment for third-degree burns is skin grafting. In John's situation, the skin grafting donor sites would have to come from the only small area of John's body that was suitable—his scalp. This meant that every piece of tissue, which would be used to cover John's body, would come exclusively from his scalp. The planned attempts at harvesting the same donor site six or more times to cover such a large area had not ever been done successfully. Survival from such significant injuries with insufficient donor sites was without precedent in the history of St. John's Burn unit.

CHAPTER 11
Why Do We Pray?

On Sunday night, Denny and I were visiting with friends on the crowded fourth floor waiting room. Amy, John's eleven-year-old sister, said that she had something she needed to talk about. She and her Dad went down to the first floor of the hospital, where they could find some privacy in which to talk. They found a bench in a corner of the lobby.

Amy started the discussion with, "Dad, you and Mom keep telling everyone to pray. What are they supposed to pray for?"

He replied, "We want people to pray that John lives."

She asked, "Doesn't God know whether John is going to live or die?"

"Sure, He does"

"If He already knows, then what is the use in praying, because whatever is going to happen is going to happen anyway?"

Denny thought to himself that this was a pretty astute point for an 11-year-old to make. He responded, "Amy, it is true that God knows what is going to happen, but He also knows how much you are going to pray to make it happen. Don't disappoint God and don't let John down."

Then Amy got a little bit tearful and said, "Dad, do you think John is going to die?"

He answered, "The doctors and nurses think so. I can only hope that they are wrong."

Amy then said, "Dad, Friday night, John and I had a fight about a TV show and I said, 'John, I hate you!' as he was going to bed." She began to sob and said, "Dad, I'll never see John alive again and the last thing I said to him was mean."

Denny told her, "That's not true for two reasons: First of all you held him in your arms Saturday morning waiting for the ambulance. He will never forget that. Secondly, you are going to see him alive, because we're going to see him right now. You can only look through the door to his room, but you will see him."

So, Amy and her dad went up to the fourth floor and into the burn unit. The person on duty said, "Mr. O'Leary, visiting hours are over and children are never allowed in the unit."

Denny gently responded, "I understand. We won't make a habit of this, but may Amy please just walk down and look through John's window. She wants to see him just one time. I want her to see for herself that her brother is still alive. We will only be a minute."

Seeing Amy's sad expression and tears streaming down her face, the nurse said, "I understand—go ahead."

Amy walked with Denny down to John's room and looked through the glass. She saw the monitors of his heart rate, his blood pressure, his respiration rate, his temperature, and his oxygen level. She saw the respirator and she saw a small figure covered from head to toe with bandages. He was hurt badly, but he was alive, and Amy saw him. She whispered into the glass window, "John, you can make it!"

CHAPTER 12
Surgery, Dressing Changes, Surgery

On Monday January 19, the first operation was scheduled to take place. We started the morning in John's room on the fourth floor, where he was transferred onto a gurney. We accompanied John, as he was wheeled through the 4th floor corridors, to the elevator, which would take us to the operating room floor on a lower level in the hospital. We touched his bandaged body, prayed for him, and told him we loved him as we walked along. Denny and I both appeared calm and confident on the outside, but inwardly we were in turmoil, with conflicting waves of profound peace and of sheer terror fighting for control. We said our goodbyes, praying that they would not be our last. He was then wheeled into the operating room. This same routine was to be repeated seemingly countless times in the coming months.

Cissy led us to the surgery waiting room in the lower level of the hospital. I picked out a corner chair facing the door, which became mine for the first operation and every one thereafter. I could talk with visitors or family members of other patients, while constantly keeping my eye on the door for the first sight of Dr. Ayvazian or Dr. Vitale.

The goal of the first operation was to remove the dead and decaying tissue from John's body in order to prepare a surface, which could successfully accept, nourish, and grow skin grafts. This surgical removal is called debriding. We received a telephone call from John's anesthesiologist, Tom Johans, from the operating room, telling us that John was under anesthesia and that the operation had begun. Tom was a member of our parish, and he and his wife Jane were friends. Both families had daughters in the second grade at St. Clement's school.

The wait was interminable. Finally, three and one-half hours later, I saw two figures, which would become all-too familiar, heading our way. It was Dr. Ayvazian and Dr. Vitale. I leapt to my feet and met them at the doorway. Dr. Ayvazian nodded and held up his arm in assurance and volunteered, "Everything went fine." He said that he and Tom Vitale had done the work of six surgeons that day and had successfully removed the dead tissue from all of the large areas and most of the smaller ones. There would need to be a little touch-up removal, which could be performed in the whirlpool.

We were relieved to learn that John's vital signs responded favorably to the strain of the surgery and that Dr. Johans was monitoring the post-operation recovery. John would be returned to his fourth floor room in approximately an hour, but would remain sedated for a considerable time. The surgery added more stress to John's already highly stressed system, but he survived.

We expressed our gratitude and asked, "What next?"

Dr. Ayvazian told us that he would like to give John a couple of days to recover from the strain of the first surgery. The removal of the damaged tissue from the large areas left John's entire body open to the threat of outside influences and the development of infection. This necessitated frequent and excruciatingly painful bandage changes several times a day.

***

The concept of bandage changing is simple enough.

Remove the old gauze and bandages, clean the wound area, apply an ointment, and replace the old dressings with fresh gauze and bandages. The complexity is that the process is extremely painful to the wound area and John's wound area was his entire body. The ointment referred to was Silvadene (silver sulfadiazine cream), which was liberally applied to the affected area twice daily to a thickness of one-sixteenth of an inch. Treatment is continued until a wound site is ready for grafting. In third-degree burned areas, the ointment acts as both an anti-microbial agent and helps to avoid sepsis in the wounded area. It can also promote healing in areas of second-degree burns.

John needed his dressings changed twice a day. The regimen required that John would soak in a tub of water to loosen the existing gauze bandages, which would then be removed slowly, yet painfully. Silvadene would be applied slowly, yet painfully, and his body would be re-covered with bandages, slowly, yet painfully. Regardless of how gentle the effort, how slow the removal, or how soft the pressure—the pain of a bandage change was agonizing. John suffered through this arduous procedure twice a day, every day.

The most tormenting and unwelcome aspect of the two-hour procedure occurred once the bandages were removed from the head. To keep the donor site free from bacteria and ready for surgery, the nurses shaved John's head during every bandage change. The scalp was always an open sore, because of its repeated use as the donor site, and the pain became intense as the razor made its way across these open wounds. John's memory of the days he spent in the hospital dulls with time, but he still has vivid memories of the dressing changes.

***

When Thursday morning came, we repeated the ritual of saying goodbye to John outside the operating room and then scurrying to the family waiting room in order to sit for hours, looking anxiously down the hall for a sign of our doctors, heading our way. In the following four months, surgical procedures occurred once or twice a week.

The separate procedures have all become a blur of waiting, hoping, praying, and engaging in mindless chatter to keep our sanity. On some days, surgery had to be cancelled because John's temperature was either too high (104°+) or too low (92°-) to safely operate. John's body temperatures wildly fluctuated, because of the lack of enough healthy skin to perform the regulatory dilation and contraction of blood vessels. John's temperature was open to the vicissitude of the ambient air or to the higher temps caused by constant fevers, which plagued him as he fought infection.

Time after time, we jumped to our feet with hearts pounding, and met the doctors at the hallway door; and time-after-time, we heard good news. Every graft that Dr. Ayvazian and Dr. Vitale placed flourished and became successfully embedded into a blood-flow rich nourishing tissue bed, which became John's new skin bit by tiny bit. This is not to say that there weren't setbacks. A myriad of problems arose during the months that followed, but the surgeries themselves were uniformly successful.

In the course of John's hospitalization, he had several debridement operations, thirteen skin graft operations, and a number of miscellaneous procedures for cutting contractures, cleaning the donor sites, treating painful sores on the scalp. In spite of the constant and uncomfortable splinting and other preventative measures, significant contractures occurred— notably in John's neck, underarm, and hip, necessitating eight surgical procedures just to provide some relief from the binding effect of the contractures. He remained in critical condition for virtually the entire course of his hospitalization.

The surgical procedure known as a contracture release requires that skin be available to place over the area being released. John required, and would have had, several additional operations to release contractures, but the lack of healthy skin that his body had available to be used as donor sites did not permit this. John would have also received additional grafting operations, but, once again, sufficient donor areas were not available.

It was somewhere during these debridement, grafting, and release surgeries, somewhere between sitting at John's bedside, walking the halls at night, praying, and begging God for a second chance at life, that I came to redefine, in my heart, the beautiful, normal, and desirable.

I came to realize that the world would not see John as fitting these categories as before, and I could not share in the world's biased judgment of my little boy.

That realization, years ago, not only freed me immensely from inner struggles, but also has opened my heart profoundly to the inner beauty of others.

CHAPTER 13
Trust Him

Trust Him when your thoughts assail you,
Trust Him when your faith is small
Trust Him when, to simply trust Him,
Is the hardest thing of all!

This became my favorite prayer, carrying me through times of desolation. In the days and weeks following the accident, Denny and I would often walk through the hospital corridors like horror movie characters—the walking dead. We were just going through the motions of life, getting up for our visits with John, smiling and accepting words of comfort from friends and family, hoping that our other five children knew that they were not loved less—John just needed us more.

Whenever we saw a parent walking with a healthy child, we wondered, "Do they know how lucky they are?"

We knew they should take that child into their arms and thank God they could do it. We urged our visitors with children to give their child a hug every day. Hold them, love them, relish them, and delight in them. Life is so fragile.

When we would see hospital visitors laughing and talking, we would wonder what could be so humorous as to make them laugh out loud. It was even a chore for us to smile.

One of our friends, in an effort to give us some consolation, repeatedly told us what an example of faith our family and we were. She said so many people were looking up to us, wondering how we had the strength to go through it.

We did not want to be role models. We had no choice. We had no desire to show the magnitude of our faith. We did not want the notoriety that was accompanying John's fight for survival. We just wanted to return home with John and our other five children and live again as a family, in a private and obscure life.

Often, when we left John's room, we wondered if it would be the last time. Yet, through all of the anguish, our faith remained with us. We continued to hope and believe that somehow John would survive. Much of the time, we could picture ourselves someday taking him home. But, at other times, a dark chill would engulf us, holding our spirits hostage in a firm, relentless grip. It was at these times of darkness, when I would say the *Trust Him* prayer over and over and over.

CHAPTER 14
Jack Buck—A Friendship Forms

On Wednesday January 21, 1987, four days after the fire, Denny sat down at the table in the burn unit nursing station to examine the medical file with regard to the extent and classification of John's injuries. At this stage, John's head and body were still swollen to twice their normal size. His bandages extended from head to toe. The only areas visible were John's singed eyelids and burned lips. John was on a respirator to assist his breathing through scorched lungs. His arms were tied out at a 90-degree angle from his body, bound to a series of weights that applied constant, uncomfortable pressure. This was called airplane splinting, because the appearance of the arm angle was similar to the wings of an airplane. John couldn't talk, he couldn't move, his eyes were swollen shut, but he could hear.

To Denny's surprise, a man, garbed in the appropriate protective mask, gown, hat, gloves, and shoe covers, emerged from John's room. With eyes moist with tears, the man in an instantly recognizable voice said to the nurse, "That poor kid is really messed up; he's not going to make it, is he?"

The nurse whispered an inaudible response while shaking her head "no" and then introduced Denny to the visitor—Jack Buck, the long-time, and much loved, St. Louis Cardinal Baseball play-by-play announcer. Jack immediately expressed an apology to Denny, if the comment about John's condition seemed insensitive, explaining that he was just dismayed by the extent of John's injuries. Denny understood because we felt the same.

Jack mentioned that the reason for his visit came at the suggestion of Red Schoendienst's daughter, Colleen. (Red was a locally well-known Saint Louis Cardinal Baseball player, manager, and coach. His daughter Colleen was a social friend of ours, living in the parish.) It was common knowledge that Jack Buck had a soft spot in his heart for children, particularly those who were critically ill or severely injured. Jack told Denny that his message to John was, "When you are up to it, after you get yourself out of here, I want you as my guest at the ballpark. I want to take you to meet (Cardinal Manager) Whitey Herzog and the Cardinal players, and I want to have 'John O'Leary Day' at the ballpark."

Over the next four weeks, Jack made it his mission to visit John regularly to encourage him and lift his spirit. Before heading to Florida for spring training, he told John that he expected him to get well enough by this summer to come to the stadium for a ball game and have a foot race with Willy McGee, the fleet-footed center fielder of the Cardinals. During the spring training radio broadcasts, Jack frequently referred to his "little friend, John O'Leary" in the St. John's burn unit and wondered whether his friend John was listening.

When the regular season started Jack continued to visit John, and he was responsible for having Ozzie Smith, the all-star Cardinal shortstop, and many other baseball Cardinals, stop by the hospital for a visit. He referred on almost every broadcast to "my friend, John O'Leary."

CHAPTER 15
Gino Cavallini—A Promise Made

On the Saturday following John's accident, we were informed by the nurses that Gino Cavallini of the St. Louis Blues hockey team was in the burn unit, asking to see John. Gino was a twenty-four-year-old, second year player with the Blues, acquired the year before from the NHL Calgary Flames. He heard about John's injury from Mike Shanahan, the Blues owner, who was a fellow parishioner in our Church. When Gino learned about this badly burned little boy in St. John's hospital, he had a strong desire to visit and try to help in some way.

The burn unit had a standing "no visitors, other than parents," order on John. Keeping visitors to a minimum was crucial because any bacteria or virus transmitted to John could be lethal. The nurse in charge told us that Dr. Vitale had approved a brief visit (subject to our consent) on the basis that Gino's interest in John could provide a much-needed psychological lift. Gino simply wanted to meet John and give him a word of encouragement.

Our initial reaction was to suggest that Gino come back at a later date. But, not knowing if we would have the gift of a later date, we decided the visit could take place. As we spoke to Gino, we sensed a heartfelt compassion, which inspired confidence that his visit could be beneficial to John. Gino was tall, good-looking, soft spoken, and anxious to help John.

His concern and empathy were evident. After some further discussion with Doctor Vitale, Gino got his chance to meet John.

Masked, gowned, and rubber gloved, Gino joined us in John's room for several minutes. John was on a respirator, could barely open his eyes, was still wrapped from head to toe, and had each arm tied out at that 90° angle in order to avoid contractures. Gino appeared very comfortable as he introduced himself to John. He told John the Blues were all pulling for him and praying for him to get well. He made a promise to John that not only would the Blues win that night's hockey game against Detroit, but ended by saying, "I am going to score a goal against the Red Wings tonight in your honor." He told John to keep up the good work and that he would be back.

Gino was a left-winger for the Blues, a very talented and tough hockey player. St. Louis Blues hockey fans loved Gino because, regardless of game circumstances or his state of fatigue, he gave everything he had on each and every shift.

Word of Gino's hospital visit, the prediction of a victory, and the promise of a goal to the injured little boy became the talk of the Blues locker room before the game. A few of the players familiar with American baseball lore began to refer to Gino as "The Babe." The Blues were playing Detroit for the second day in a row, having lost in Detroit the night before.

Gino did not score in the first period, but the Blues did gain a lead. He did not score in the second period, while the Blues maintained a one-goal advantage. As the third period progressed, Gino's team mates, well aware that time was running out on Gino's promise, stood up and shouted words of encouragement.

Then it happened! With just minutes to play, Gino

intercepted a pass, skated to the blue line, and released a vicious slap shot, which screamed past the surprised goalie, to put the Blues ahead by two goals. Tears of joy welled up in Gino's eyes and in those of the other players aware of the pledge. The famous story of Babe Ruth hitting the homerun in Yankee stadium for the sick child had been duplicated in a hockey arena. In fact, a Ruth homerun in any given game was statistically much more probable than a Cavallini goal on demand. The final score was Blues 5 Detroit 3. Gino was named the first star of the game.

On the following day, Gino and many of the other Blues players came to the hospital. A visit by so many players was totally out of the question, but Gino was allowed to again mask, gown, and glove. He told John that he and the team had come to the hospital to present Gino's Blues sweater (what the player's call their uniform jersey) worn the night before, when the goal was scored. The jersey was autographed by the entire team. There was a slight trace of a smile on John's burned lips.

The Blues went on to win the Norris Division in 1987 and Gino kept in close contact. Over the period of the continued hospitalization, Gino visited dozens of times. Following surgery for the placement of skin grafts on John's back, he was required to lie face down on his stomach for more than two weeks. The mattress had an opening in it so that John could breathe more comfortably in his facedown position. The hole also permitted John to look at the floor, but that was all he could see, while waiting for the grafts on his back to heal. When he came to see John, Gino saw that John was not able to look up, so he just sat on the floor under the opening, entertaining and encouraging John. He would call John "superstar" and tell him that everyone Gino talked to wanted to know one thing, namely, "How is John doing?"

When Denny and I expressed our gratitude to Gino, he responded, "Don't thank me. It has been my privilege to spend time with John. He has taught me about courage, strength, and perseverance, beyond my imagination."

CHAPTER 16
You Saved Me

J im was allowed to visit John for the first time in February. John was still not able to talk because of the tracheotomy. We had developed a system of communication whereby Denny or I would point at a letter on an alphabet board, and John would make a clicking sound when we pointed at the correct letter. Thus, we spelled words as John clicked his approval. It was slow, at times frustrating, but it worked.

When he saw his brother, John's face lit up with joy. Jim was equally joyful, but shocked at the devastation to his little brother, even obvious through the head-to-toe bandages. Jim quickly rallied, smiled, and said, "Hi Chester" (Chester was a nick name for John that the kids used, usually in conjunction with referring to John as "Little Chester, such a fine fellow.") John initially hated the name and the teasing, but eventually learned to live with it, and finally, secretly enjoyed it.

John clicked for his alphabet letter board and quickly spelled out the first word, starting with a "J" and an "I." We watched with rapt attention as John then clicked out his message. After the "J" and the "I," we pointed in anticipation to an "M" to which John readily agreed. He then clicked for a "Y," with our then guessing an "O" and a "U," to which John quickly clicked confirmation. Next came an "S" an "A" and a "V" from John, with our "E" and "D", followed by an "M" and an "E." John anxiously spelled out to his brother "JIM, YOU SAVED ME."

Tears of thanksgiving welled up in the faces of both brothers. This was something John had wanted to tell Jim since January 17. John knew if Jim had not acted so quickly and decisively, he wouldn't have lived to even get into the ambulance.

Jim responded, "John, I may have helped, but you are doing the hard work. Keep it up." Jim changed the subject to, "I hear you had some interesting visitors."

John nodded "Yes."

"Who?" asked Jim.

To which John spelled, "J-A-C-K—B," with Jim guessing, "Buck." John smiled proudly. John then started "spelling" the name of Gino Cavallini, which Jim correctly guessed after the "G" and the "I." Andy Van Slyke took a little longer. Jim stayed a few more minutes, asking questions that could easily be answered "Yes" or "No" by a nod or shake of the head. Jim left with the knowledge that, although still in critical condition, John seemed to be making definite progress. Jim whispered to me outside John's door, "Mom, if that were me in there, I would have wanted to die."

CHAPTER 17
Three Steps Forward, Two Steps Back

Although on many days, signs showed that progress toward survival was definitely taking place, most days were filled with constant worry and wonder. For example, one day we saw a doctor whom we didn't know, giving instructions to the nursing staff. She turned out to be a pediatric pulmonary specialist who was treating John for pneumonia. He had a very high fever, was listless, and the critical condition was even more so. On a different occasion, a physician, identifying himself as an infectious disease specialist, came to speak to us about his plan for getting control of a life threatening bacteria that had entered John's body. We didn't know about the pneumonia, we didn't know about the infection. We only knew what Cissy Condict frequently reminded us—that with a critical burn, no problem is "unusual or unexpected."

***

On one occasion after about 14 weeks of hospitalization, we went into John's room and he was hallucinating about the "fish in his boat" and the "muscles on that guy over in the corner." There were no fish and there was no guy. John could not hear us and seemed to be in some sort of a trance. Doctor Ayvazian said that this was in the nature of a coma caused by the continual stress and strain on John's mind and body.

The conscious mind, in effect, decided to take a vacation from reality. Despite the many horrendous unknown concerns we had continually faced since the start of John's hospitalization, this was, perhaps, the most difficult for me to accept or to fully comprehend. Dr. Ayvazian told us that this condition could last for days, weeks, or even months. I was beaten down by this strange phenomenon, causing my heart to pound with fear, anger, and frustration. At this stage, Denny and I were ready to take our own vacation from reality.

***

One evening, John was in intense pain. He was always in substantial discomfort, but this was something different. As the night wore on, his discomfort increased. He begged for help with darting glances from Denny to me and back again. We were frantic. We not only couldn't help, we didn't even begin to know what the problem was. We asked the nurse on duty to come in and check everything. She said everything was in order. We pleaded with her to look again. She finally noticed that the chart for the urine output either had not been updated or he hadn't urinated in about nine hours, in spite of constant hydration. We were petrified, fearing that it was the beginning of kidney failure, which we learned weeks ago would be a definite possibility with a severe burn. Fortunately, as his nurse rechecked everything, she discovered that there was a clogged line. His bladder was ready to burst. The blockage was cleared and John breathed an audible sigh of relief; it was times like this that reinforced our commitment for at least one of us to be at John's side whenever possible.

***

One of the worst days came in connection with some

paperwork that we were given to review. For each operation, we had to sign a parental consent form. Dr. Ayvazian said they had waited as long as they could to save John's fingers. Most of the finger sections had turned black and they had to be removed. Denny was given a consent form that talked about something along the lines of "digital debridement and amputation"

Denny refused to sign at first and said, "I just can't do it. I just can't."

The nurse said she understood how he felt, but the form had to be signed. She looked in my direction when Denny spoke up, "I don't want you to sign such a horrible thing, Susan. I'll do it."

Placing his signature on that form was the most difficult moment of his life.

When we saw John after the procedure, he was heartbroken. He said he would never be able to catch or throw a ball again, write, drive or even take care of himself. We assured him that he would, but secretly had misgivings of our own. Very small pieces of a few fingers were all that were left. They remained on contractured hands that were left with very little movement. Both thumbs were amputated completely.

CHAPTER 18
Memorable Moments

Mirror Mirror on the Wall

One day in mid-February, 1987, we went into John's room for a morning visit. He seemed unusually discouraged. He was still on the respirator and unable to talk, but he was getting a bit stronger and could communicate by head movements.

I asked him if something was wrong and John nodded, "Yes."

I asked him if it was part of his body and he again nodded, "Yes."

"Your legs?"

"No."

"Your stomach?"

"No"

"Your chest?"

"No"

"Your head?"

"Yes"

"John does your head hurt?"

"No"

"Your head doesn't hurt, but there is something wrong with it?"

He nodded affirmatively "yes."

I got an idea and said, "John, you think your face is burned like the rest of your body, don't you?"

He nodded "Yes" and tears began to form.

I said, "John your face is not burned, except partially on one side. The middle part around your forehead, eyes, nose, mouth, and chin is beautiful!"

He shook his head in disbelief, "No."

Then I asked, "Have you been able to look at your face in a mirror?"

John shook his head, "No."

Would you like to?"

"Yes"

Denny went out, got a mirror, and brought it back. I held it up and said, "See?"

He saw that his nose was intact and there was not scarring of significance on the main part of his face. John visibly breathed a sigh of relief.

John had seen the devastation to his hands, arms, torso, and legs and naturally thought that his face had met the same fate. After seeing his face in the mirror, he was relieved.

This is Heaven?

John recalls waking up in the hospital the first morning after the swelling in his head and body abated. He remembers distinctly seeing "St. John's" on his sheets, his pillowcase, and on the blanket. He didn't know where he was, but reached the conclusion that he must have died and gone to heaven, where he became "St. John," with his own personalized bedding. He said he was glad to be a saint, but heaven did not seem to be all that he had hoped.

Truth or Consequences

On the day after the surgery to debride the digits of his fingers, John was very discouraged. He said, "Mom and Dad, they keep doing things to me. What are they going to do next?"

I said, "John, I don't know, but there will be no more surprises. I'll tell you anything that I learn and will answer any question that you have truthfully and completely."

John said, "You will?"

I answered "yes" and I could sense the wheels turning in his little mind.

"So, Mom, no matter what I ask, you will answer and tell me the truth?"

"Yes, John."

"No matter what?"

"Yes, John."

"You promise?"

"Yes."

Then John asked his question, "Mom, is there a Santa Claus?"

Any questions?

Dr. Tom Johans, John's anesthesiologist, grew very close to John over the many months of surgery. He would always solicit and answer John's worried questions, because surgery in spite of the frequency and number never became "old hat," with the success of each operation vital. Before one of his last operations, John was laying on the gurney waiting to be transferred to the operating room. Dr. Johans came over to John and said, "John, here we go again. Do you have any questions?"

"Yes, Doctor"

"Shoot! What is your question?"

"Doctor, how much money do you make?"

We listened intently to see what our physician friend would answer.

SUSAN AND DENNY O'LEARY

Those aren't lungs

One evening, John had once again succumbed to pneumonia, while scheduled for yet another surgery the following morning. An X-ray had been taken around midnight and Denny and I were anxiously waiting in the hall at about 1:30 A.M. for the results that would determine whether surgery was a "go" or not. As we turned the corner of the corridor, an intern in a white coat, holding a set of X-rays, approached us and said he had good news. We eagerly followed him into the consultation room where he could post the X-rays for viewing and explain the results.

As he held the film up to the viewing screen, he pointed out that there was not a complete fracture, which caused me to reply, "Doctor, I'm certainly not a radiologist, but that sure doesn't look much like a pair of lungs to me."

He was terribly embarrassed when he determined we were not waiting for the results of a broken hip X-ray, and we were not the "Jones family."

We said, "Don't worry! Anyway, we are happy for Mrs. Jones."

CHAPTER 19
No Pain, No Gain

The purpose of physical therapy is to retain or recover muscle, joint, ligament, and tendon flexibility and function. An extensive regimen of therapy began in the hospital while John was still in extremely critical condition.

Dr. Ayvazian wanted him to be able to move to the extent possible, should John somehow survive the severe burns. A lack of therapy would have resulted in a lack of ability to function in any real sense. The contracting muscles would have pulled John into a life-long immobile fetal position. The decision was made that, although the therapy would be extremely taxing on an already over taxed body, the risk was worth the effort should John defy the odds.

John's "normal" heart rate while hospitalized was approximately 120 beats a minute. His heart was racing, trying to send blood, nourishment, oxygen, and healing to all portions of his body. There were many difficult moments, as we watched John's heart rate increase to well over 200 beats a minute during the therapy sessions. Denny and I feared that his brave little heart would just give out—but it didn't.

John's skin, muscles, tendons, and joints were stretched and manipulated so as not to become totally frozen with concomitant loss of all function. The pain was excruciating, as every joint of John's back, arms, legs, hands, and fingers were bent, stretched, and twisted.

John had a physical therapy session twice each day. For the first several months, the therapy was given to him in his bed in the burn unit. For the last month or so before discharge, he went to the lower level of the hospital to the physical therapy room. John dreaded these sessions. His joints continued to be manipulated and his muscles were stretched. The pain was agonizing and progress seemed minimal.

CHAPTER 20
Why Me?

Sometime in late March or early April, John was no longer in need of a respirator, so the tracheotomy was changed to a talking trach; this could be used for anesthesia administration during surgery and would permit John to talk normally once again. We were all very pleased to dispense with the alphabet board/clicking form of communication.

One of the first things John did after regaining the ability to talk was to say, "Dad, I have a question that I have been thinking about since the day of my accident. Why did this happen to me?"

Denny said, "John, that is such a hard question to answer. At times life is terribly unfair. Things happen. Horrible things, like what happened to you, are just a part of being alive. Mom and I really can't give you an answer."

That night, while we were talking about our day, Denny came back to John's question and said to me, "Susan, there must be a better answer than what I told John. His question was just like Amy's on the night of the accident, when she asked me, 'Why do we pray?' I wasn't satisfied with my answer to her, either. There are so many questions. Sure things just happen, but isn't there some reason? Does God play any roll in our lives? You and I know that he does good things in answer to prayer, but if He sends good things, does God ever send bad things. I never thought so, but I'd like to come up with a better answer to 'why me' and 'why pray?'"

Over the next week or so, Denny thought, read, and prayed about it. He reached some conclusions, which he shared with me:

'Why me' is an age-old question. Most of the pat answers do not make much sense. Certain people believe that everything that happens 'happens for a reason'—although they are quick to admit that they usually don't know what the reason is. Others believe that God purposely sends bad things to us, just to see how we will respond.

There are common expressions such as 'God won't send you problems greater than you can handle' and 'when He closes a door, He opens a window'. In my opinion, none of this correctly depicts the manner in which God chooses to be involved in our lives. It's also not plausible to conclude that if someone has strong faith, they will suffer great hardships.

It would be logical for us to receive in direct proportion to what we deserve—maybe we wouldn't like what we got, but if what we received were a function of our conduct, good or bad things would at least be predictable. The good would receive good things and the bad would receive bad things.

The only problem is that things don't work that way. It is well known that bad things do happen—to good people, to bad people, and everyone in between—but so do good things. The Bible says that it rains on the just and the unjust, but doesn't say "why."

The best known query of the "why me?" question comes from Job in the Old Testament book of the same name. Job was a rich landowner, who lived seven hundred years before Christ. The opening line of the story describes Job as a 'blameless and upright man who feared God and avoided evil.' He was then in good health, had a nice family, hundreds of livestock, and was extremely wealthy.

God had a conversation with the devil about Job, Satan saying that it is no great thing to fear God when things go as well as they have with Job. Satan told God if you take away some of those things Job has, he will blaspheme to you in your face. God agreed to let Satan act, as long as he did not actually kill Job.

Suddenly, Job had a huge reversal of fortune. His children were killed, his property stolen, his animals died, and a horrible skin disease attacked him. Job desperately wanted to know "why me?" His friends all told him, "You must have done something wrong and now God is getting even." Job knew this wasn't true. He remained faithful and he continued to pray. He told God and his neighbors, 'Naked I came into the world and naked I will return. Blessed be the name of the Lord!'

Job continued to trust in God and eventually became even wealthier than before. This is a rich story, which teaches about the rewards of remaining faithful through any problem or crisis. It also stands for the conclusion that God allows certain things to happen, even though he might not send it, but it doesn't answer the threshold question of 'why?'

There is also a much-discussed "explanation" in various writings making reference to a cloth tapestry, having a good side and a bad side. The bad side has imperfect threads and uneven knots—these represent the hard times on earth and what we see from our vantage point. The other side of the tapestry is what God sees and what we will see in heaven—a perfect tapestry without a blemish. This makes a nice story, but certainly doesn't help answer "why" the bad side, "why" the knots!

I know that God did not send this horrible accident so that John would be tested or to see how strong he is, or to repay him for anything he did, or we did, or anyone else did. God did not send it at all. He did know it was going to happen and He allowed it to happen—because he seldom interferes with the law of nature. He was as saddened by the accident as we are.

God doesn't play games with his people. Jesus told us repeatedly about His Father's love for us. A God, who would please himself by jerking the strings of a puppet, is not a truly caring Father and could not claim to be a 'God of Love.' God is incapable by his nature of being anything less than fully and unconditionally loving toward His creatures, whom He made in His own likeness. My first conclusion, then, is that God does not send bad things to those we love, because He loves them even more.

The reason that John got burned was because his actions inadvertently set in motion certain natural laws of gravity and physics. God permits the consequences of the natural order, but He will stay with us and comfort us if we call upon His name in times of distress!

My second question is. "If God doesn't send bad

things, does He truly send good things, or does He just 'stay out of it?' " If He does not get involved in some fashion, then our prayers of petition are an utter waste of time. People have been praying for millennia, have dedicated their lives to prayer, and constantly try to develop a strong prayer life. Is this foolish? Why do we pray to God?

The reason we should pray arises form the simple premise that God, to be God, must be Love. This loving God desires to send good things to those he loves, just like we want to provide them to our children. The conclusion is inescapable that the Lord responds positively to prayer—often not in the way that we request, but always in a manner which can be readily recognized and fully experienced.

This still leaves the original question, namely, 'why me?' The only answer to 'why me' is 'why not me?' If one chooses to defy the laws of nature, or if one's body wears out, or if someone is in the wrong place at the wrong time, bad things will happen, whether to me or to others, to my family or to their families. At these times, we must turn to the Lord with unwavering trust that He will help us.

The Gospels are replete with examples of the power of faith-filled prayer. The miracles performed by Jesus are not told by the Evangelists to show that Jesus is divine. They are there to demonstrate that the power of God will be made manifest and available to those who ask for it.

Every miracle that Jesus performed was in some way connected with a radical act of faith. The kingdom of God is intended to begin for us here on earth. Jesus, through example, was telling the disciples and us to call upon our heavenly Father in times of distress.

Many times, it seems that our prayer is not answered in the way we would choose. Perhaps we don't get the "cure" that we want, but that does not preclude our receiving the inner "healing" that we need. At times, we will hurt, at times, we will suffer, but in the darkest times, we should take comfort from the following promise:

The wrongs and injustices of earth will be righted. God will measure out our tears, which He has kept in His bottle, and not a single one will go unnoticed. He who holds all reasons in His hand will give us the key that makes sense out of our most senseless sufferings. And that is only the beginning! (Anonymous)

CHAPTER 21
Homecoming

One day in late April, Doctor Ayvazian wanted to talk with us. So, we went into the usual "private room." He closed the door and astonished us by saying "I think there is a good chance you may get that miracle for which you have been praying."

I gasped, then smiled and hugged Dr. Ayvazian, and asked if he was saying that John was going to live.

"Well, there can be no absolute guarantee. John remains in critical condition, because there is a considerable amount of healing necessary for him to be out of the woods. We have at least several more grafting operations in store for large areas without skin covering. We need to get an additional harvest of donor site from the scalp, which we have taken and used five times. There may not be sufficient donor sites available to fully cover areas of his backside. The grafts must all take. Meanwhile John is still subject to system shutdown, infection, pneumonia, and numerous other concerns. He is still in critical condition, but he is making remarkable improvement. If all goes well, he may go home by June.

As we practically floated out of the room with tears of joy in our eyes, we chose to ignore everything else we heard except "John is going home." The date was established as Saturday, May 29th. We circled the date on the large wall calendar in John's room and marked off every day with a big X.

A week before the big day, we were told that John would be discharged as anticipated, but could not go home as scheduled. He would be moved to another facility for continued burn care. We were shocked and knew that John would be devastated.

I asked incredulously, "Why?"

The answer involved the necessity for continued painful dressing changes twice a day, which would take hours, accompanied by cauterization at the skin edge of the open areas to promote spreading of the grafts. A silver nitrate stick must be applied to all edges of the large open areas, each application feeling like giant bee stings.

I responded to the news, "We promised John he was going home and that is where he's going when we leave here. He's been through so much, I can't stand by and break his heart."

I asked if the nurses would teach me to do the bandage changing and to apply the nitrate stick. Permission was reluctantly given and I attended a number of training sessions. It was painful to simply watch. How would I be able to inflict this pain on my little boy? I developed some serious misgivings about my promise, but, John remained on course to be discharged and going home.

The big day came! Denny and I arrived at the hospital on the morning of May 29, 1987, with a wheelbarrow filled with 24 bottles of champagne and a hundred tubes of the candy, appropriately named "Lifesavers", to give to our burn unit lifesavers.

On the way to the hospital, we stopped at the grocery store and were in the checkout line, when the man behind us saw the champagne and said, "Must be quite a celebration!"

I told him that we were taking our son home after 4 1/2 months in the hospital and that initially, he was given virtually no chance of survival.

He asked a few questions, and then added, "He must be a special boy. I am going to see to it that a tree is planted in Israel in the name of 'John O'Leary'." He explained that this was the way in which Jews in the United States can give a meaningful remembrance, and at the same time, fill a monetary need and a beautification effort in Israel.

We entered the hospital for the 132nd consecutive day, but this day we were excited beyond belief. The weather was glorious—bright, clear, 70 degrees, and a light breeze. Nature cooperated with a perfect backdrop for John's homecoming.

John was excited, but apprehensive. He couldn't walk, except for a few staggering steps; he couldn't hold anything in his hands; he had large, painful, open areas without skin covering; his head throbbed at recent donor site areas; he would have to come to the hospital twice a day for physical and occupational therapy; he would have to come to the burn clinic every Saturday morning for a medical review of his condition; he was weak and in pain, but he was going home!

The occupational therapy department gave us some Velcro eating utensils to be strapped to John's wrists. I thanked them but said, "John will not have to eat with spoons tied to his wrist. We will teach him to use his hands and to hold his utensils, so he can feed himself. He'll learn."

We wheeled John out of the fourth floor burn unit to the cheering and tears of his nurses and others on the floor, who were well aware of the significance of the day—a day that no one, other than perhaps John, truly expected to occur. We rode the elevator onto the main floor and wheeled John down the large main corridor to the exit door, while many others wished him well. All the wonderful faces that had lovingly cared for and encouraged John were there to show support.

Denny gingerly got John into the station wagon, shut the door, and got in the car, saying, "John, you did it!"

We drove the five-minute ride home at a much different pace than John's last journey between home and the hospital. John asked if there might be anyone at home, besides family. I said, "Probably."

When we rounded the turn on our street and our house came into view, John saw a large gathering on our front lawn and on the yards of adjoining neighbors. Included were many of John's classmates, their parents, his teachers, his siblings, his neighbors, his cousins, his grandparents, his godparents, his coach (who swore "Johnny will make it"), and lots of family friends. There were balloons, banners, posters, and welcoming shouts of joy and jubilation. John took a wheelchair ride to the front porch, where months earlier he had lay in Amy's arms at the point of death, waiting for an ambulance. An impromptu receiving line quickly formed, with one person at a time greeting John with a hug, a kiss, an atta-boy, a smile, and tears. He still had to climb that steep mountain a step at a time, but he was home.

"Johnny made it."

His coach was right.

CHAPTER 22
The Mass of Thanksgiving

During the early weeks of John's hospitalization, Denny and I vowed that if John survived, we would have a Mass of Thanksgiving. It was with jubilation that we scheduled the Mass to take place at St Clement's church on Thursday, June 18. This was three weeks after his discharge from the hospital. Without any effort at publicizing the celebration or sending invitations, we were pleased that word-of-mouth spread to the point that the church was filled with more than 600 friends and well wishers, including doctors, nurses, therapists, ministers, priests (including Cardinal Carberry, retired archbishop of St. Louis), John's classmates carrying banners, the gospel choir from St Bridget's inner city parish, and a host of other friends, acquaintances, and some strangers, all of whom were moved by John's progress.

John agreed to read the first scripture passage from the Old Testament. After the opening prayer, the congregation sat down to listen to the word of God. You could feel the surprise when John stood up and haltingly shuffled to the ambo. He was wearing splints on his neck and arms, along with the terribly uncomfortable Jobst elastic garment on his entire body. His hair was starting to grow back, following the recent use of his scalp, once again, as a donor site for grafting. Denny helped John up the single step, as he slowly worked his way to the microphone.

John lowered the microphone to his level, looked out at the congregation, then down at the Bible and read in a soft, high-pitched voice:

The LORD is my shepherd; I shall not be in want.
He makes me lie down in green pastures;
He leads me beside quiet waters.

He restores my soul. He guides me in paths of righteousness for His name's sake.

Even though I walk through the valley of the shadow of death, I will fear no evil, for you are with me; your rod and your staff, they comfort me.

You prepare a table before me in the presence of my enemies; you anoint my head with oil; my cup overflows.

Surely goodness and love will follow me all the days of my life, and I will dwell in the house of the LORD forever.

An almost supernatural silence fell upon the church, as this faith-filled little boy read the ancient words about a faithful God. Tears of thanksgiving for John's life, tears of joy for how far he had come, tears of sorrow for how far he had to go, all flowed shamelessly. Everyone in attendance realized in their hearts that they had suffered less and complained more.

At the end of Mass, Denny got up and made a few comments. He stood in the center aisle, thanked everyone for attending, and for his or her role in helping John get to this point. He started with the doctors and nurses who provided outstanding medical care. He thanked those who had opened their homes to us, all those who so lovingly prepared and delivered meals to us—night after night. He thanked those that had cared for our children when we couldn't; those who provided rides for our family; those who had cleaned, helped reorganize, and set up our home when we moved back in.

He thanked those who had ministered to us by their presence, when we were in the hospital. But, most importantly, he expressed extreme gratitude for the blessing of everyone's prayers. We are of the firm belief that if one person had said one less prayer, John might not have survived—he was that close to death.

It was five months to the day, that Denny had stood in the same spot with many of the same people, when there was no cause for optimism, hardly a reason to hope, and with only a flicker of faith. He had asked the Lord to hold John in His loving embrace, keep him safe, heal him, and someday return him to his family.

Someday had come! John was back home. He still had a steep climb ahead, but with the love of his God, the support of his community, continued skilled medical treatment of his doctors and his own special indomitable spirit, we believed that John would make it back to full health and find happiness.

CHAPTER 23
Take Me Out to the Ballpark

In addition to spearheading visitation by sports celebrities, Jack Buck initiated the anonymous mailing of baseballs individually autographed by one of the Cardinal players. The baseballs first arrived in early June 1987, days after John was discharged from the hospital. The sender made it a requirement that John write a thank you note to the player in question, acknowledging the gift. Due to finger amputation, John initially could only make an X. With the ongoing assistance of occupational therapists, he later became able to write in shaky, and large, barely legible letters. John did not like to write those thank-you notes, but he liked to receive autographed baseballs. So, he wrote the notes.

On July 10, 1987, the long anticipated baseball game with Jack Buck arrived. John went to the stadium wearing white pants, a red shirt, his hot, tight, and very uncomfortable Jobst body suit, a neck splint, several arm splints, a Cardinal hat and an enormous smile. John, who was still unable to walk any distance, was transported by wheel chair for much of the distance, but gamely hobbled along side Jack whenever possible. He went to the dugout with Jack during batting practice, and talked inside baseball with Cardinal Manager Whitey Herzog.

John talked to a few of the players before the game, asked slugger Jack Clark to hit one out of the ball park, and happily sat beside his friend and mentor, Jack Buck, for what turned out to be an extra inning ball game. John wouldn't consider leaving until the game was decided, even though the hour was getting late. As midnight came and went, the rest of his family in a nearby private booth, were beginning to feel like hostages. Then, in the bottom of the 13th inning, Jack Clark stepped up to the plate and launched a game-winning homerun. Those fans still remaining cheered as they headed for the exits, while John and Jack Buck headed to the dressing room to congratulate the team. John was ecstatic, as was Jack—shedding tears at the enjoyment of this special little boy, who defied all odds.

Later that summer, Jack was inducted into the baseball hall of fame in Cooperstown, New York. He was given the opportunity to address those gathered in Cooperstown, as well as those in the television audience. With his unique wit and great pride, Jack introduced his family, he reminisced about his friends and the good old days of baseball. He boasted about his team and the giants of broadcasting with whom he was fortunate enough to have shared the microphone. He referred to his own job, as the Cardinal broadcaster, as the best job in all of baseball. He then mentioned his young friend John O'Leary, calling him "as gutsy a person as I had ever met."

As John's parents, we were well aware of John's unceasing courage, but to have Jack Buck not only mention John, but also to do so in such superlatives before a national audience, deeply touched our hearts.

CHAPTER 24
One Step at a Time

At the time that John came home from the hospital he was confined to a wheel chair. He could only hobble short distances, could not bend his knees, arms, or wrists. He had to be carried up or down the stairs. As part of his therapy, John was required to go to sleep each night with an electric machine hooked to one of his legs and alternately hooked to the other leg every two hours. The machine forced knee flexion and extension, which was extremely painful at the peak of the flexion. Denny would get up three times every night to alternate the machine attachment from one of John's legs to the other. John, at times, would whimper, but would not ask for relief or for the right to sleep without pain. He had much earlier decided he was going to do whatever it took.

John continued to require physical therapy from St. John's twice a day for months after the hospital discharge. The therapy was essential in attempting to keep the wounds and scars from tightening, which would decrease, impair, or negate John's mobility. The pain caused by the therapy was agonizing. It was so intense that the therapy at St. John's was administered in a closet and a washrag was stuffed in John's mouth (with his consent) to muffle the agonized screams. John would, at times, cry in fear and trepidation, on the ride to the hospital. He would ask for prayers to relieve the pain, but he never once said, "Don't make me go."

He continued to fight his way back, one step at a time.

Seeking advice from a knowledgeable friend, we were able to find and bring to our home, independent physical therapists to augment the St John's therapy. We eventually were able to discontinue the trips to the hospital, but the therapy sessions continued seven days a week. John's primary home therapist, Maureen Sheehan, had a wealth of experience in dealing with the peculiar limitations of burns. She also loved John from the beginning, working with him very intensely for more than a year. Although Maureen hated the pain that she caused John, she knew that she was without option, if he were to make progress.

It was not unusual to see Maureen mentally anguished and crying as her little patient was crying from physical distress. Although Maureen had compassion for John, she also had a passion for restoring function. She continued to stretch and extend the tight, scarred skin, the frozen joints, and stiffened muscles.

Maureen brought John a bicycle, with a metal stand that converted it into an exercise bike. The exercise on the bicycle was intended to give John some strength and flexibility in his hips, knees, and ankles. She began the quest of attempting to help John pedal in a full circle. Successfully pedaling a bicycle would indicate that significant progress was made in the stretching of John's hips, knees, and ankles. John's scars were so thick and the muscles so tight that at first he could not rotate the pedals more than about 14 inches or 90 degrees out of the required 360 degree circle. It seemed an impossible task. Maureen persisted, and John, despite the pain, did his best.

Finally, one day in November 1987, about 10 months after the accident, John climbed on the stationary bicycle with a look of determination. He pushed hard and readily got past the 90-degree mark, he pushed harder and got to about 140 degrees—just a few more inches. John knew that if he got to 180 degrees, the 360-degree point was merely the other side of the same coin. He emitted a grunt of effort, a groan of pain, and a yelp of victory. Success! He did it! He finally made the full circle with the bicycle pedals.

The next day, John made several more circles and then marked improvement began. The sessions remained painful, but under Maureen's strict tutelage, and with a lot of encouragement from his siblings, John learned to walk, he learned to climb stairs, and he learned to run—awkwardly, haltingly, but proudly.

The following summer, the O'Leary family vacationed in Copper Mountain, Colorado, due to the generosity of two wonderful families in our parish. One of the families insisted that we christen their brand new GMC conversion van in the Rockies, and the other graced us with the use of their lovely condo in the heart of the Copper Mountain resort. John joined us on a 14-mile bicycle ride in the mountains, traveling from Copper Mountain to Frisco. The best part of the bike ride was having John with us. The second best part was that it was 14 miles downhill! It was a ride that just a few months earlier, none of us dreamed John would have been able to make.

CHAPTER 25
Whatsoever You Do

I was homeless and you took me in;
I was hungry and you fed me;
I was thirsty and you gave me to drink;
Naked and you clothed me;
Lonely and you visited me;
Ill and you cared for me.
(Matt 25: 48)

This passage from the gospel of Matthew addresses many of the amazing and selfless things done for the O'Leary family by the St. Clement's and St. Louis communities and beyond, during the year following John's accident. Every human need that we had was addressed, usually before we knew we had the need.

These actions embody the kingdom of God on earth, working through its many and diverse members. We received prayer and support from Whites, Blacks, Hispanics, and Asians; from Catholics, Protestants, Muslims and Jews; from men, women, boys and girls; from married couples, single friends, divorced, and widowed; from the extremely wealthy to the very poor; from doctors, nurses, aides, therapists, lawyers, accountants, architects, builders, teachers, students, salespeople, clergy, religious, ministers, secret service agents, carpenters, plumbers, hairdressers, executives, secretaries, waitresses, stay-at-home mothers, and many others.

This listing is not merely a random catchall. We can recite a true story about each and every one of these categories—for most, multiple stories and examples. Every one of these individuals was essential for our journey to have the right ending; every single act done, every prayer uttered was itself important and salvific.

We were not aware of many of the activities, at the time they were done. I am sure we still do not begin to know of many other kindnesses, which permitted us to focus on what we did know—our little boy was in critical condition, which was sufficient to occupy our minds, hearts, and spirits.

St. John's Gospel ends with the comment that "these things Jesus did, but He also did other things, which if all listed would exceed the world's storage capacity." Similarly, others did the following things for us, but these things do not even begin to encompass all.

When I was homeless you took me in.

While we were staying at my parents' home, a friend told me that we had been offered a five bedroom home, two blocks away from our church and school, by a family we knew and were certainly friendly with, but had no close relationship, by any means. Generosity to this degree continues to amaze me. This incredibly kind couple was spending the month of February in Florida.

We moved into their home three weeks after John's accident and for the first time since January 17, we experienced some degree of normalcy. The owners of the home decided to extend their trip an extra two weeks, so that we could move directly from their house to our refurbished home in mid-March.

When I was hungry you fed me

One of our friends approached me the morning after the accident, asking what she could do for us, in addition to prayer. I told her it would be helpful if she would take a dinner out to my Mom's house, where our family was staying. She took a meal that evening as requested. She then organized meals to be delivered to the family from a large list of St. Clement volunteers, five nights a week for the next eight months—initially, to my parents' home, then to the home supplied near the school, and finally, to our home, once we moved back into it. These 160 meals cooked with pride and delivered with love, proved that there were a lot of good cooks in our parish; but, more notably, they proved that there were a lot of good people.

Ill and you cared for me

There was a perception that John would need a great deal of blood to survive. One of our friends started a blood drive program for John's benefit. He also handled the scheduling logistics. Well over a hundred wonderful people gave a unit of blood to the St John's blood bank. Many more, including the entire junior class at DeSmet High School, were on the donor list and offered to give blood for John, if needed. Our son, Jim, was a member of the junior class at DeSmet and this was the school's way of offering support.

Naked and you clothed me

Our home had been extensively damaged by the fire and smoke, and was uninhabitable for months. The thick, brown, billowing smoke, had been sucked through the entire house by the heating system and literally permeated every room, every closet, and every drawer. Every item of clothing had to be taken out, washed, and returned. Without worrying us with the details, some of our friends went into our home, emptied all of our drawers and closets, emptied the pantry and the kitchen, cleaned the bathrooms and the basement, and made an inventory of everything they touched for insurance claim purposes. All of our rugs, curtains, bedding, towels, and clothing had to be taken to appropriate cleaning agencies to remove the soot, dirt, and that terrible stale smoke odor.

***

One anecdote involves a very dear lady in our parish who wanted to help the O'Learys in this difficult time. She had shared with a mutual friend that she wasn't particularly comfortable babysitting the children and that cooking was really not her thing, either, but she could wash clothes like nobody else. Most of our clothing had been removed for cleaning, but there were seemingly hundreds of white socks gathered in the bathroom upstairs. My friend dropped the basket of socks off at this lady's house one day and, by the next afternoon received a call from her. She had washed, dried, and dumped the socks on her dining room table and, after searching for more than half an hour, she realized that she could not find a mate for any one of the socks. She was dumbfounded and said, "Susan's family always looks so beautiful and together on Sunday mornings. I can't believe they don't have socks that match."

When Denny heard this humorous story, he called the dear volunteer and said the answer to her dilemma was simple. He told her, "We wash the right foot socks on Monday and the left foot socks on Thursday. We then mate them on Friday, but this time the socks had apparently gotten separated."

Situations like this would give us both momentary relief from the stark reality of the day.

***

John was not fully covered with skin when discharged from the hospital, and large areas on this backside, back, and one leg were open wounds requiring a bath and bandage change each day, which could take up to two hours. Our next door neighbor's daughter, a nurse, came to our home every other morning and a nurse friend in the parish, who had five young children of her own, came to our home every other afternoon for several months to help with the tedious bandage changes, and application of the silver nitrate stick.

Lonely and you visited me

We had hundreds of visitors who came regularly to the hospital. There were so many that one of our "caretakers" spread the word to come less often and stay less time so that we could get some quiet time. Many of the visitors have been previously described, but a few more deserve mention.

***

One of the Jesuit brothers at DeSmet High School came to the hospital's fourth floor waiting room every day for three months, just to be present and to help solve any question or problem that would arise. Don would sit there silently if we wished, or be talkative when we wanted.

One evening well after midnight, I was at the hospital alone with John. I left his room feeling afraid, depressed, and questioning my ability to keep going. As I walked out of the burn unit, trying my best to contain my sobs, there was Don, just sitting there—waiting. Somehow his presence gave me the reassurance that some type of continuity existed.

***

One of our nieces also came to the waiting room virtually every day to help, or to just be present. She is a quiet, sensitive girl, who understood what it meant to just be there for someone.

***

Gene Stallings, who was then the coach of the St. Louis Football Cardinals, stopped by the hospital to see John on a half-dozen occasions, always referring to John in his comforting Texas drawl as "you little rascal," as he offered words of encouragement. He was especially sensitive to John's pain and injuries, because Gene also had a son who required special care.

***

One day, I was going into the burn unit to visit John, when I noticed that our pastor was outside John's room getting garbed in mask, gown, and gloves for a visit. Father was very sick, in fact, dying from cancer. He got to John's door and the nurse said, "I am sorry Father, but we are doing a dressing change and it may take a couple of hours. The priest sat down and said, "That's OK. I'll wait!" He sensed that he didn't have much time left and he wanted to give John his blessing.

***

John was required to go to physical and occupational therapy at St. John's initially for two visits a day, later reduced to one per day. A group of ten mothers in the parish volunteered and met all of our transportation needs. Day after day, week after week, they pulled into our driveway on schedule with a smile and some encouraging words for John.

Miscellaneous Acts of Love

John's medical costs, including surgery bills, exceeded on average $4000 per day. Our hospitalization and medical insurance involved a national plan with a $250,000 family lifetime limit, which would be consumed long before John's treatment could be concluded. One of Denny's relatives had set aside a sum of money sufficient for the college education of his three children—but the entire amount was offered to us if John needed it for his care or treatment. Incredibly, the amount of the group insurance was raised for the entire national group from the $250,000 limit to $1,000,000 midway through John's hospitalization. This falls, also, in the category of miraculous.

***

John's godparents generously presented him with an expensive TV Nintendo game with lots of buttons to push. We thought it was impractical and potentially frustrating, considering the nature of John's hand injuries. To the contrary, it was rewarding, because John learned how to adapt, and before long could beat any adult and most children. This helped satisfy John's innate need to compete.

***

My sister-in-law was another daily visitor, coming to the house or to the hospital or wherever we needed her. For months she volunteered to do those things that no one else wanted to do. She also developed a close relationship with Laura, our youngest, who was going through a difficult time when I was home so seldom.

***

My sister, who had small children at home, supported us through constant intercessory prayer.

***

My mother took charge of keeping track of our kids and their schedules. She made sure they were all accounted for. Mom seldom had a chance to visit the hospital during the first month or two—she had to do her worrying and praying from her home.

***

My father took care of all of the insurance details, replacing all of the contents of our home; cleaning and replacing damaged items from the farthest upstairs bedroom to the darkest basement corner. He made a meticulous inventory, with Jim's help, of all of the items stored in the garage from a riding lawnmower to a package of thumbtacks.

***

Several of Denny's sisters left their families and came from out of town, staying with our children at the borrowed home for more than a week each.

***

A good friend who enjoyed nothing more than an ice cold Coca-Cola gave up Coke for the rest of her life, as a sacrifice for John's benefit. I can't imagine a sacrifice to that degree for a friend's child. This gentle friend, with her profound closeness to the Lord, touched our lives deeply—and seventeen years later, she continues to do so.

***

My father was a chain cigar smoker. He never had another cigar after January 17, 1987, but never would say why.

***

Different families graciously took our girls on vacations that first summer, which freed them from the routine exposure to therapy, bandage changes, and the painful procedures, which John had to endure. Cadey went to Florida, Amy and Susan went to Wisconsin, and Amy was fortunate to have a second trip, this time to Florida. These wonderful families generously covered all of the expenses for our girls.

The test of time

Real friendship is shown in times of trouble; prosperity is full of friends. (A. Kuyper)

There are those certain people who are graced with a gift of sensing what someone needs and knowing the time to deliver it. To have such a person in your life, especially in a time of tragedy, is certainly God's blessing. Mary was present the first hopeless day. She continued to support me through the darkest hours, and was there on our front lawn at John's triumphant homecoming, holding the banners she made. She had become my communication to the outside world, John's greatest fan, my interior decorating consultant (when I simply had no interest in making a decision on color or content), our children's loving supporter, and a continual source of prayer and encouragement. How fortunate I was!

A Doctor's Prayer

One afternoon in the fall, I walked into St. John's physical therapy department to pick John up after his grueling afternoon session. One of the therapists told me that a party was going on upstairs in the burn unit for Dr. Vitale who was moving from St. Louis. John and I were asked to attend.

When John walked into the room, all of his old friends

were excited to see him. While John was the center of attention, Dr Vitale took me aside and said, "Susan, can we talk for a minute." He went on to say, "I usually make a point of not mixing my prayer life with my medical treatment, but when I saw John in the emergency room when he first came in, I was extremely concerned by the severity of his burn. I called my mother, who has a devotion to the Infant of Prague, and I told her there was a little boy who had been brought in that morning, who I desperately wanted to save, but didn't think I could. I told her about your family and I asked her to pray for John." Dr. Vitale's eyes grew moist with tears as he said to me, "Susan, she has prayed for John every day for the last eight months. I just wanted you to know."

Additional Prayers

John received more than a thousand Mass cards, letters, notes, and get-well cards. We received dozens of phone calls weekly and more love, care, concern, and goodness than we could ever have hoped for or imagined. St. John said in his gospel, *"If every one were written down, I suppose the world itself could not contain the books that would be written."* (John 21:25).

Books of John's visitors, helpers, prayers and supporters, might not fill the world, but they would be plentiful.

CHAPTER 26
Glenn Cunningham: Never Give Up!

Fourteen months after John's accident, in March of 1988, we received a telephone call that a man by the name of Glenn Cunningham was coming to St Louis to complete work on a video being produced about his life. Glenn was a 78-year-old, nationally prominent, motivational speaker, who was badly burned as a child. He had heard of John's story of survival from a family friend in Saint Louis, who produces motivational films. Glenn planned to be in town for some final work on a video of his achievements, which was titled *Never Give Up*. He wanted to make sure that John was going to do more with his life than be content with survival.

Glenn Cunningham, who traveled to St Louis from Arkansas by means of an old pick-up truck, was best known for winning a silver medal for the mile run in the 1936 Olympics held in Munich, Germany. His ability to compete, much less win a medal, was especially notable, because Glenn's legs had been severely burned as a seven-year-old child. The accident occurred at his schoolhouse when a can of gasoline was mis-marked as a can of kerosene, resulting in a violent explosion and deep and disfiguring burn wounds. His doctors believed it would be advisable to amputate both of Glenn's legs at the knees, because of the extent of the injury. There seemed to be no hope that Glenn's legs could be saved and the doctors were concerned that the dead tissue could lead to further complications from gangrene.

Although she understood that he was not expected to walk again, Glenn's mother pleaded with the doctors not to remove the burned legs. She begged them to give Glenn a chance to regain use. They reluctantly agreed, much to Glenn's relief. The doctors cut away the dead areas from the lower portions of the burned legs, doing what they could to save living tissue. Although it took more than a year before Glenn could walk even a few steps, he fought his way through intense pain, learning first how to walk and then to run. Glenn, like John, exceeded all expectations. He actually became one of the best runners of all time.

Glenn trained hard and made his high school track team. By his senior year, he set a world prep record for the mile. In college he won several Big-Six mile runs, two NCAA titles, and numerous AAU titles. He was named the best amateur athlete in the United States. After graduation he was asked if he would like to try to earn a spot on the United States Olympic track team. He not only made the team, but finished fourth in the 1500 meter run in the 1932 Los Angeles Olympics, and won the silver medal four years later in Munich.

As remarkable as an Olympic Silver medal is, Glenn's lasting contribution was of a totally different nature. He had a special concern for children lacking support from a loving family. Glenn and his wife had a 40-year ministry directed toward the needs of troubled young people—kids that had dropped out of their own families, and had nowhere to go and no one to care about them.

The Cunninghams lived on a farm in Arkansas. Over the course of many years, they opened their hearts and home to young people rejected by society. There was a total parade of guests in excess of a thousand children, teenagers, and young adults. Most of the visitors would appear at their door unannounced, but were always welcomed to come in. After hearing the house rules and consenting to abide by them, the strangers became family and would typically stay for a period from several months to several years. Genuine warmth existed between the youths and the couple.

There would usually be 80 or 90 young people present at any given time. As long as the family member adhered to the family rules, studied hard, or worked diligently, he or she was welcome to stay. Each member of the family was expected to perform chores. Although there were never any formal court adoption proceedings, most of the young boarders called Glenn "Dad" and his wife "Mom" and considered them as such years after they left the farm.

Glenn told Denny and me that there were many times when he had no idea where the next meal for his huge family was coming from, but it always worked out. He said that the Lord was looking out for him. Glenn's favorite prayer was the Bible verse "Allow the children to come unto me."

He recited one instance when he had 87 hungry mouths to feed and was totally without money. When Glenn went to get the mail that particular day, he found an advance deposit check for a speaking engagement to which he had agreed months earlier. The Lord's presence in his life was certainly reflected in his dealings with others.

Glenn told us that he would like to spend a few minutes alone with John so that they could have a man-to-man discussion. Glenn and John went for a walk together, John hobbled with his burns, and Glenn slowed by his 78 years. Glenn, who had so many years of knowing and understanding young people, told John his story and asked John to explain his goals and ambitions.

John confided to Glenn that he was beginning to be

somewhat discouraged. After a year and a half, John still walked with a noticeable limp and couldn't run very well. He also told Glenn how he missed shooting a basketball, catching a football, kicking a soccer ball, and the like. Glenn gently reminded his new little friend, "John, your continued life was a miracle given to you by God. With His help, you overcame incredible odds. Think back about how far you've come and then picture yourself doing whatever you desire to do. Visualize it. Don't be satisfied with mediocrity. You will be able to do whatever you believe you can do. Set high goals and expect high achievement. Don't ever give up on your dreams!"

When they came back from their walk, we asked Glenn to stay at our home for dinner. He thanked us, but said he had to be getting back to Arkansas. He pulled out of our driveway and headed back to Arkansas, leaning out the window to remind John to "Never give up."

John seemed both moved and motivated by the experience. Unfortunately, it turned out that Glenn had made his last trip. He died two weeks later at his home in Arkansas, surrounded by his wife and a houseful of children.

CHAPTER 27
Carlos Pappalardo. MD—Hand Surgery

There is one additional doctor whose effort and skill has been instrumental in John's successful transition to fully functional living. This doctor is Carlos Pappalardo, a plastic surgeon, who worked closely with Dr. Ayvazian in situations involving burns that required reconstructive surgery. Dr. Pappalardo was confident, caring, and had substantial experience with burned hands and other reconstructive surgery. He started monitoring John's condition and progress after several months in the hospital, hoping that Dr. Ayvazian would somehow be able to leave a donor site available to provide skin for John's badly burned hands. Dr Pappalardo was also the surgeon who had assisted in a number of John's contracture release surgeries.

John's hands were burned so badly that virtually all finger function was eliminated through injury and amputation. Basically, John was left with three fingers to the first digit on each hand and no thumb. The fingers were locked in place by contractures, a web-like phenomena in which tissue bonds and binds to adjacent tissue following a severe burn.

It is our thumbs with the opposing action that gives us the dexterity to carry things, grab things, and, in general, to obtain meaningful hand use. Without a thumb, human hands would work little better than paws. It was functioning thumbs that Dr. Pappalardo most wanted to construct for John. He explained to us and to John that he would make a deep cut into the gap between the missing thumb and the partial first finger, and then free up the part of the thumb deep in the hand for use as an opposing mechanism. Some repositioning of the muscles would be required, together with trying to make a "palm" that could be opened to whatever extent possible. The task was further complicated by the contractures, which not only held the fingers in place, but which also effectively closed each hand into a ball.

Although confident in his ability and anxious to help John gain function, Dr. Pappalardo said that other surgeons might have a different approach to the problem, suggesting that time was not a factor and that we should seek other opinions.

We received many suggestions from interested friends and family members. We started off by talking to a doctor at Cardinal Glennon Hospital, which was affiliated with Saint Louis University Medical School. The meeting was surprisingly brief. We arrived and were ushered promptly into a patient treatment room. The doctor walked in, greeted us, looked at John's hands, and said, "Wow, your hands are really burned badly! I don't have experience with such an extensive injury. You need a world class surgeon."

He recommended a surgeon he knew in Shriners' Hospital for Children in Cincinnati, Ohio. The Shriners have world-renowned burn unit facilities in both Cincinnati and Dallas, Texas for treating burn injuries to children.

Within a few weeks, we had an appointment scheduled in Cincinnati. Denny, John, and I drove to the Shriners' hospital to meet with the recommended hand specialist. Upon entering the room, the doctor said, "I see that you've been burned; but I've seen worse."

He made this comment, presumably to show his experience

based upon only a quick glance, before even examining John. The doctor inquired as to whom we were considering in St. Louis. We said, "Carlos Pappalardo" to which the doctor tersely replied, "Never heard of him."

We questioned the doctor in some detail as to what he would do and why. His approach was similar to that of Dr. Pappalardo. The doctor was confident, experienced, and brash.

Our third appointment was with hand specialists at Barnes Hospital in St. Louis, which is a teaching hospital associated with Washington University Medical School. The Barnes facility is nationally acclaimed, for its medical research and being in the vanguard of improved and new treatments. The Barnes' medical team of doctors had a totally different approach. They suggested the removal of two toes from each of John's feet to be utilized for the construction of a longer finger with an opposing thumb. They showed us photographs and films of toe-grafting operations, which were fascinating and promising for function. There were, of course, no guarantees that the toes would take at the hand relocation site and not just be lost. John didn't want to cut off his toes—fingers were bad enough.

After making the circuit and considering our options, we decided to place John's hands in the skilled and loving hands of Dr. Pappalardo. When told that the Cincinnati physician did not recognize his name, Dr. Pappalardo in response, quipped, "That's funny, I've never heard of him either."

Surgery was scheduled for several months later, and suddenly we were back at St. John's hospital ready to begin the reconstruction of John's hands. Dr. Pappalardo intended to start with the right hand, which was John's dominant side. We found ourselves following along with John on a gurney toward the operating room and greeting Tom Johans as he prepared to administer anesthesia—just as we had done more than 20 times before.

Although the risks to John of losing his life were no greater than normal surgical risk, we found ourselves particularly tense on the morning of surgery. This was a critical day in John's life. There would be little else that could be done to achieve hand function for John, should this operation fail. We prayed that the Lord guide every move of Dr. Pappalardo, as he departed from a brief meeting with us to the operating room.

I took my familiar seat in the surgery waiting room, looking intently for a new figure to come within view of my corner chair. After six hours, Dr. Pappalardo came out of surgery. He smiled and made the initial comment, "The result will be as beautiful as an Italian sunset." The surgery was a success. So was the following surgery to the left hand. Within limits, John can twist, hold, lift, open, cut, and give a handshake. His hands are not what they once were, but the thumb opposes the finger and they work. John accentuates the positive about what he can do, refusing to complain, or make excuses about anything for which he needs a little help. What John can accomplish with his hands is truly amazing—but, again, so is John.

CHAPTER 28
As Good As Ever

When John was discharged from the hospital, he had missed the second half of his fourth grade school year. We didn't believe that he would be strong enough to go back to school in September 1988, and we knew he couldn't accomplish the make-up schoolwork, while in pain, and busy with the therapy schedule. We gave some serious consideration to simply holding John back a year and letting him start fourth grade over, with a new class. He was strongly opposed, because his friends meant so much to him.

As has so often happened, the Lord provided us with help in an area that we had not yet even realized a need. A young woman in our parish, an experienced, state certified, tutor, who had three small children of her own, volunteered and insisted that she wanted to work with John all summer to help him catch up by the start of fifth grade. This incredible young mother worked with John twice a week for the entire summer to help get him ready to rejoin his class.

Although John was capable academically, he was not even close to being physically ready to begin school in September. Because of John's impaired physical condition, he qualified for educational assistance through the Special School District. This was how Cathy Collins entered John's life.

I'll never forget John and Cathy's first meeting. I was concerned about how a stranger would react to John's injuries.

Cathy walked into the breakfast room where John was sitting, gently touched him on the arm, and said, "John, you really have been through a lot."

She commented on the pain he must have endured, the effort it must have taken, and the determination he obviously had. I left them alone to begin the session and within minutes I heard bellows of laughter coming from the kitchen classroom. That began a semester of school like John had never experienced, with a teacher whom we will never forget.

Most of the school work was oral, because John's badly burned hands were not yet capable of holding a pen in a way that would allow him to write more than a couple of letters. Dr. Pappalardo had not yet performed the required hand surgery. With the help of his dedicated tutors, John made up the missing school materials and caught up with his class. Although extremely apprehensive, he was ready to return to his school in January 1988, a year after the explosion. The early days back in school were difficult, because John was barely able to walk or write. He was in constant pain, but persevered.

People would frequently ask, "How's John doing in school?" and we would always answer, "As good as ever!" The response to this would be "Great!"

We wouldn't volunteer that "as good as ever" was not as good as it sounded. John always had an interest in knowing and understanding things, but he was not overly motivated to extend himself any further than necessary in the pursuit of grades.

John's team had a new soccer coach, a father of one of John's friends. The coach told John to come to practice when he could and when he felt up to it. He would play either way and would have his starting position as soon as he felt ready. John was still weak, couldn't run very well, and was not able to play more than a small portion of any game.

In the third game of the season, one of the boys on the opposing soccer team was guilty of a handball in the penalty area, giving the St. Clement team the opportunity to kick a penalty shot. This is a one-on-one kick against the goalie. The coach, who could have chosen any player for the kick, looked over and said, "John, go get us a goal."

John, with an artificial confidence said, "You can count on it!" Then partially bent over, with pencil thin legs, and an uneven gait, John whistled the soccer ball over the goalie's outstretched hands.

The remarkable thing is not the goal, but the coach letting John have the opportunity. So many coaches are motivated to win at any cost, starting in grade school, overlooking a child's sensitivity and potential. John's coach today still feels good about his decision and we feel good about the coach.

High school days came and went. John was not able to play high school sports, but did play sandlot games with his friends. His grades were about a "B" average—as good as ever. The academic highlight occurred in John's keyboarding class. He received an "A" on his report card for the semester. When we went to parents/teacher night, Denny asked the instructor whether John could truly type at an "A" level. The teacher said he actually would have gotten a very solid "B," but he looked at that kid, looked at his effort, and decided 'what the heck' if John doesn't deserve an "A," no one does.

When it came time to teach John to drive, he proved to be a quick study and did a competent job of holding onto the steering wheel and making turns with limited hand function. We went with John to get his driver's license and we all had concerns that the examiner might decide that John needed a special driving apparatus of some type. John showed that he could do it, and was given a license without restrictions. He is an excellent driver, without any accidents and without any tickets (at least from what he's told us).

John had a wonderful group of friends, both boys and girls, whom he hung around with, went to dances and parties with, and lived the life, ostensibly, of a typical high school student. The teenage years, alone, can be painfully difficult, much less with the challenges that faced John.

He did confide in me "Mom, I have a lot of girl friends, but do you think I'll ever have a girlfriend?"

This question tore at my heart.

John graduated from DeSmet High School and decided to attend Saint Louis University where he would live on campus. We were concerned about whether John would find the right roommate, when he received a call from an acquaintance that was a year ahead of him at Saint Louis University. He asked if John would like to room with him the following fall. This was the first time that John would leave the shelter of his family and try to make it on his own. What a difference that telephone call and invitation meant to John and to us.

John developed a large circle of close friends and enjoyed fraternity life and his college days to the fullest, while his grades continued to be "as good as ever." His quick wit, delightful personality, and I-can-do-anything attitude helped him draw friends like a magnet.

John graduated from Saint Louis University with a degree in finance. His siblings, grandparents, Denny, and I attended his pre-commencement ceremony. The dean started the diploma delivery by announcing that he would first call alphabetically those students who graduated *summa cum laude*, followed by the *magna cum laude's,* followed by the *cum laude's,* followed by the rest of the graduates. Accordingly, we sat back in our chairs expecting a long wait.

When the *"summa's"* reached the "O's," we heard "John Ryan O'Leary, *summa cum laude.*"

We knew there was a mistake. But it was not merely a mistake. Upon entering the graduation hall, John had taken his name card, printed *summa cum laude* neatly upon it, and deliberately stuck it into the wrong stack. Following John's designation as a *summa cum laude* graduate, we cheered as loudly as did the parents of the biochemical engineer with the straight "A" average—in fact, we cheered louder.

CHAPTER 29
Jack Buck—Encore

The relationship between John and Jack Buck continued and grew stronger. Jack referred to John fondly in a series of television specials and interviews. He marveled about John's tenacity in his autobiography, *That's a Winner.* Jack made a standing offer for John to come to the Cardinal announcer's booth any time he was attending a ballgame, which John continued to do several times each summer through high school and college.

When John graduated from Saint Louis University, we invited Jack and his wife Carole to a family graduation party. Jack and his Cardinals had a game that evening, which prevented his attendance. When we arrived at the restaurant, we noticed a beautifully wrapped package on one of the tables. The manager told us that Carole Buck had dropped off the gift earlier that evening. When John opened the present, he found the Waterford crystal baseball awarded to Jack in Cooperstown, New York by the Baseball Hall of Fame committee at the time of his induction. It was engraved with an inscription of the event. The package was accompanied with a simple note "John, this baseball means a lot to me. I want you to have it. I hope it will mean a lot to you."

It was a gift of incomparable meaning and value to John.

When Jack died in the summer of 2002 at age 77 from complications arising from Parkinson's disease, John was interviewed for a television special on his friend. John said that "losing Jack was like losing an out of town grandparent whom you love, but don't see as often as you'd like. It hurts."

Denny and I will never know the extent to which Jack's kindness and interest in this little boy was responsible for giving him the extra incentive to keep fighting during the darkest times.

John gives Jack credit for teaching him that a simple act of kindness can mean so much. John recounted his joy at receiving the autographed balls during his first summer of recovery, which John related on the television interview. "I learned that one person can affect another's life by doing simple things. Jack just took a little interest in me. He sent me balls, making me realize that my actions can affect someone else's life."

John was inspired to start an annual Parkinson's disease fundraiser in honor of Jack Buck and for the benefit of Denny, who was diagnosed with Parkinson's in 1993. In the first two years of John's "Toast for the Cure" held at Humphrey's Bar near Saint Louis University, John raised more than $25,000 for the Michael J. Fox Parkinson's Foundation. How touched Jack would have been with the efforts of this "gutsy kid" in his reaching out and helping others.

Denny and I have never been certain as to the exact reason for John overcoming this devastating injury. We are confident that the miraculous hand of a loving God was actively involved. We also believe that the prayerful love of family and friends was a crucial element. John's personal strength and tenacity were critical, but we cannot overlook the affection and attention showered upon John by his friend and supporter Jack Buck, because there can be such a fine line between success and failure, hope and despair, life and death. We are eternally grateful for Jack's role in helping John not cross over that line.

CHAPTER 30
Beth, I Hear You Calling

John, like many young men, was not anxious to talk to his mother about his social life. However, we heard through the grapevine—consisting of a Saint Louis University student to her parents in Colorado, to their good friends in Colorado, who were also our good friends, that John was dating a Saint Louis University coed named Beth Hittler—and that she was pretty.

Conceding that he had established a friendship with Beth, John denied that there was any more to it than that. We met Beth for the first time at our daughter Amy's wedding in the summer of 2000. The next time we saw Beth was five months later, when John brought her to Arizona to join us at a family wedding. A client of Denny's provided us with his five-bedroom home on a private country club golf course in Scottsdale, Arizona. We were impressed with Beth's sweetness, beauty, and, even more, her tenderness toward John. All of our kids liked her and she joined right in the family banter.

Later that summer, Amy joyfully, but tearfully, recounted to me a conversation that she and Beth had while talking in the hot tub in Arizona. Amy asked Beth if it was difficult for her to deal with John's burns and scarring. Beth told Amy that when she first met John, the extent of his injuries was overwhelming. However, she also immediately noticed that he was an amazing person with a handsome face and a great sense of humor. Beth told Amy that as time has gone by, "I don't even see scars anymore—just John."

One day after John brought Beth to a birthday party at our house, Denny asked him whether he and Beth were getting serious. John admitted that they were. When asked if he was going to marry this girl, John responded that he wasn't. Denny wondered whether that meant not now or not ever.

John said, "Just not right now."

They dated for an additional year or so, when John surprised us with an excited telephone message a week before Christmas. He said, "Mom and Dad, I asked Beth a certain question tonight and she said, "Yes."

We could feel John's jubilation coming through the telephone wires.

At the rehearsal dinner the night before her wedding, Beth went to the microphone and told the courtship story from her perspective as follows:

John and I met my freshman year, his junior year, at Saint Louis University. I was friends with other guys in John's fraternity, Phi Kappa Theta. I was invited to a fraternity dance and was 'assigned' to John O'Leary as one of his five dates. This was the first time I met John and we ended up dancing with each other to the song *"Sweet Caroline"* by Neil Diamond. I saw John a few other times during the school year. He asked me to the spring Phi Kap dance and I knew that I had found a good friend.

I asked John to come to a sorority dance in the fall of my sophomore year. He brought flowers, which I thought was sweet of him; but viewed him only as a friend. A few months later, we went to a Neil Diamond concert and enjoyed it completely, in particular, the live performance of *"Sweet Caroline."*

At a fraternity Christmas party a few months later, John began to hint to me that his feelings for me were growing strong. I told him I was not ready to be anything more than friends. I just was not sure of my feelings for him. When John invited me to his spring fraternity and graduation parties, I knew that we would remain friends. I told John I was so happy to have him as a friend and gave him a framed picture of the two of us for graduation. I began to feel some sort of connection growing. I always thought of him, and even began to imagine us dating.

John came to my house in January of my junior year for my 21st birthday and mentioned that his sister Amy was getting married. I hoped that he would ask me to go to her wedding. Later that year, he invited me to be his date. I was thrilled.

During the fall of my senior year, John would call me once in a while, which made me happy. We would see each other occasionally at Humphrey's bar and would always dance to *Sweet Caroline* when it was played. I realized that I wanted to be more than friends with John. I knew I had to tell him how I felt.

We met for dinner at Café Napoli and I told him what I needed to say. Two years later, at the same restaurant, John asked me to marry him. Words cannot explain the joy that John had brought to my life. I said, "Yes!"

CHAPTER 31
The Top of the Mountain

The wedding plans were made. The dress selected. The invitations mailed. John and Beth invited more than 400 guests to the special event and the list could have included hundreds of other admirers and friends.

Mama said there'd be days like this

I spoke after the wedding Mass with the encouragement of my family, including the blessings of John and Beth. I expressed my unbridled joy at the resolution of a concern that I carried heavy in my heart for the last 17 years, a concern which John spoke of to Denny while he was still in the St. John's burn unit. These were my words:

> Beth and John, when you chose this date for your wedding day last December, Dad and I felt that there couldn't have been a more meaningful time for the two of you to marry, than Thanksgiving Week. As you celebrate this Sacrament of Marriage, I know you have to feel the incredible love, support, pride, and thanksgiving from the hearts of all these people in your lives—400 of whom are here rejoicing with you tonight. You are a special and unique couple.

> John, it has been 17 years since the terrible accident that brought you so close to death. During the five months you were hospitalized and in such

critical condition, your father and I turned you completely over to the Lord with the simple prayer that against all odds you would be healed and returned to us—and you were.

I'm sure you remember one afternoon toward the end of your hospitalization, you and Dad were alone in the room, and Dad said, "John, everything is going to work out fine. And you, only 9 years old said, "That's easy for you to say—you've got a wife, a family, a job and a home. I may never have those things."

Through persistence and hard work you have taken care of the job and the home, leaving only the prayer for the love of a good wife. Beth, this is where you fit in. As I look at you tonight, I remain overwhelmed by your beauty, humility, and grace. You are the person that John has been searching and praying for his whole life.

Denny and I were also praying for you, Beth, for all those years—we just didn't know who you were then. You have become the center of John's life as his wife, completing the hope of a little boy, expressed so long ago. We could not feel happier or more blessed. And so, Beth, as Denny and I gave John to the Lord 17 years ago—tonight we give him to you. May God continue always to bless you both with His grace and continued presence.

He's incredible

At the wedding reception there were several toasts, including one by Jim, John's brother, and best man. Jim eloquently covered how far John had come since the accident and what a remarkable man he is today. Jim's message was as follows:

I have the honor of being John's best man. I have known him his whole life as my brother and my friend. I can remember before the accident when John was little, playing basketball, baseball, and football with him in the back yard. He was the best little athlete that I had ever seen or even heard of. John didn't know the meaning of quit; John developed such a drive to succeed, which continues to the present.

After the accident, John's determination increased tenfold. He had the courage to fight impossible odds to overcome the condition that was given to him. He taught himself to play the piano. John quickly became the best ping-pong player in the O'Leary family, a family made into good ping-pong players by the lousy weather, which so often plagued our vacations. I couldn't beat him, even if I cheated, which l tried to do every chance I got, because when you lost to John, he let you hear about it.

Without the ability to use wrists or fingers, he could compete with us on the basketball court. He shoots by somehow balancing the ball on the back of his hand while pushing up hard underhanded. He became one of the best Bubble Hockey players in the state of Missouri. After winning the St. Louis regional tournament, followed by the Eastern Missouri and Southern Illinois regional tournaments, John and his partner flew up to New York last year, as guests of the sponsor Anheuser Busch. They made it to the national quarterfinals. He is truly incredible.

A few years ago, I asked John to go out to Colorado so I could teach him how to ski. By the end of the second day, he was flying down the black expert slopes, without sticks and without fear.

Father Pieper, our Pastor, tried to teach John to water ski on Lake Litchfield behind a 38-year-old boat named "Num Nums." John tried to get out of the water by balancing the hard handle attached to the ski rope against the back of his hand at the wrist. A large amount of pressure and pain would develop as the boat pulled away. John had tried to hold on until the boat pulled him out of the water, without success, 15 or 20 times. Dad told him, "John, it just isn't worth it; give up"

John replied "It's worth it to me."

Moments later, he got out of the water, stayed up on the skis, and conquered yet another obstacle. John can now water ski with no problem. He is just an amazing individual.

More important than athletic success is John's caring commitment to his relationships with family and friends.

You could not ask for a better, son, friend, or a better man. Everyone who knows John considers him an inspiration and a hero. But, even a hero needs a hero of his own—someone to lean on for guidance, support, and love. That hero is Beth.

I lived with John for several years and I was able to watch their relationship grow and flourish. I saw how happy John was to be around Beth. I saw him use his same drive and determination to win Beth over. Beth is a caring, compassionate beautiful young woman. They both truly need, love and take delight in each other.

Please join me in a toast to the newlyweds, "John and Beth, may God grant you everlasting happiness, love, health and wealth—a wealth of family, of friends, of children and years."

Did I ever tell you you're my hero?

John gave the last toast to a standing ovation. John wanted to thank his doctors, nurses, and friends. He wanted to make sure that everyone knew that his brother saved his life. He wanted to tell Beth he loved her. This is how he said it,

Jim, that was perfect—just like I wrote it.

They say that you lose your masculinity when you get married. That's not exactly true—you start to lose it when you get engaged. I didn't know anything about dresses, trains, veils, flowers, programs, and the like. I didn't know that women had times in the month when they could be moody and rude to you without any reason; and I didn't know they could change it to any time they choose.

I just wanted to say a few words of thanks to the people who mean a lot to me. There is a table of nurses here, who I want to thank for all they did for my family and me. They were with me twenty four hours a day—often not even leaving my bedside, as they would monitor my vital signs in times of medical crisis. They gave me care, support, and helped me maintain the will to keep fighting.

I would also like to thank the doctors who worked with them: Dr. Vitale, who is in New York, Dr. Johans, my anesthesiologist, and Dr. Ayvazian, my burn surgeon. Dr. Ayvazian is the best surgeon I could ever have hoped for, but as good as he is as a doctor, he's a better human being. I am so fortunate to have gotten to know him better over the years—and, how many kids have their own private anesthesiologist?

The person who gave the doctors and nurses the opportunity to do their jobs was my brother and best man, Jim O'Leary. For those of you that know the story, you know that Jim is the hero, not me. Jim, I appreciate every single day what you did for me and I wanted to say it here in front of everyone. Cheers to you, Jim, you are the real hero.

My four sisters, Cadey, Amy, Susan, and Laura have supported me, helped me, and encouraged me from the beginning. You will always be very special to me.

I want to thank my grandparents for everything they did for me. When I was growing up, my friends must have thought that I had very old parents, because my grandparents were at every school function that I participated in. My grandfather died in January; he is not here in person, but he is here in our hearts.

My parents are perfect role models. I want to be like them when I am a parent. They are selfless and 100% behind their children in everything that they do. Mom and Dad, thank you for that you have meant to me and for all the things you've given up for us.

That's 18 "thank-you's" down. There are 390

to go, so this will last for four hours or so. Get comfortable!

I want to thank all of our friends who are here tonight. Beth and I have thirteen tables. You are all remarkable people; you are exceptional friends, and fun to be around. Thank you for all you continue to give to us each and every day.

I want to thank everyone who came in from out of town. We have people here from California, Texas, Louisiana, Colorado, Kansas, South County, Arkansas, Minnesota, Michigan, Illinois, Indiana, Tennessee, Georgia, Florida, Rhode Island, Connecticut, Massachusetts, New Jersey, and New York. We know it is not inexpensive to travel. Beth and I are appreciative and flattered.

The Lammerts and the Hittlers made me feel part of their families from day one. I will look forward to getting to know you all better. You have been so welcoming and loving.

I saved the best for last. Beth, you are an exceptional person. You have so many wonderful qualities. You are beautiful, compassionate, and completely giving of yourself. I love you today. I loved you from the day I met you. I look forward to a long and happy life. I am the luckiest man in the world.

***

John climbed to the top of that treacherous mountain, where he met Beth, his beautiful bride. At their wedding reception, surrounded by family and friends, the bride and groom again danced to *Sweet Caroline*. There was a second standing ovation at the reception, accompanied, I know, by thunderous applause throughout the heavens. We kept faith in God, who kept faith with us. Our journey with John has ended; Beth and John's journey has just begun. They have each other and are truly blessed!

EPILOGUE
(written by John O'Leary)

Character cannot be developed in ease and quiet. Only through the experience of trial and suffering can the soul be strengthened, vision cleared, ambition inspired, and success achieved.
(Helen Keller)

I stepped out of the shower tonight and looked for some time directly into the mirror. The mirror had been covered in the steam from the hot water and I could barely make out my own image. Through the fog, I could see the dark brown of my hair and a normal looking body mass that made its way from my hair to the bottom of the mirror. Nothing was clear; no body parts, either identifiable or unique. It was peaceful to stare at myself and not see anything that would make me any different from anyone else. Just the blur of a person—as I imagine a person with cataracts must see all of life

I stared at this illusion of myself for some time—so long in fact that the fog in the room and the steam on the mirror began to dissipate. Then I began to see myself for who I really was. I realized steam, makeup, or material items might trick me into believing that I am someone that I am not. But, when the air cools, and the steam disappears, the makeup rubs off, or the money is all spent——we are left with who we really are. It is up to each person to find his or her way and purpose in life and after 23 years, I am still very much searching for my own deeper purpose.

The shower is over, the steam is beginning to lift— what will I find when I really look into the mirror? I would like, by the time the fog has completely cleared, to look directly at myself into a perfectly reflecting mirror—and to love what I see. **Excerpt from John's journal, June 2002**

Years ago, my mom asked me how I felt about her writing a book about all of our experiences beginning with the morning of January 17, 1987. I told her that I didn't want to live in the past and couldn't see how anything we went through, both good and bad, could be of interest to anyone outside of our immediate family. I was not comfortable with others seeing all we went through and giving them unfettered access into our personal family life. I did not tell her not to start the book, but I wasn't motivating her to continue her writing of it, either.

Years later, as the chapters were continuously read to me over the phone or e-mailed to my house, two realities were unveiled to me. The first was that the book was going to be written and the other was that the real story wasn't about me or my parents or even our experiences along this journey, but instead about something much more meaningful and universally important.

The importance of the book and the miracles within do not solely concern the successful fight of a boy to survive his serious injuries against all odds. It isn't about the struggles that take place in the hospital, whether in the patient's room or in the hearts of his parents. It isn't about the family's attempts to remain together after the loss of their home. It isn't about suffering and perseverance. The book is actually about God's unseen and unexpected magnanimity that is revealed to us all.

It is during our own suffering that God's grace most shines upon us. The friends and family who we most loved were empowered with strength they were previously unaware of possessing. People we had not even encountered, entered into, and were able to touch our lives in ways that will forever have significance.

Overwhelming Odds is about the countless people who gave, sacrificed, and prayed so much as to eventually affect the survival, and then life, of a child. The importance of the book is to reveal that by giving of ourselves, we can become part of someone else's miracle. And the real miracle is that we are all given the ability, opportunity, and mandate to do so.